JOURNEY THROUGH
AUSTRALIA

By the same author

NOVELS

Just Relations
Captivity Captive

POETRY

Selected Poems
The Collins Book of Australian Poetry (ed.)

JOURNEY THROUGH
AUSTRALIA

Rodney Hall

JOHN MURRAY

© Rodney Hall 1988

First published 1988
by John Murray (Publishers) Ltd
50 Albemarle Street, London w1x 4bd

Typeset by Butler & Tanner Ltd
Printed and bound in Great Britain by
Butler & Tanner Ltd, Frome and London

British Library Cataloguing in Publication Data

Hall, Rodney
Journey Through Australia
1. Australia—Description and travel—1981–
I. title
919.4'0463   DV105.2

Cased: ISBN 0-7195-4495-5

Note on the Eureka flag (*on title-page*): This flag, with its formal representation of the Southern Cross, was hoisted over the Eureka Stockade on the Ballarat goldfields in December 1854. It has been used on many occasions since to signify defiance against repressive authority, and faith in an independent future.

CONTENTS

Contents

ILLUSTRATIONS

Illustrations

Illustrations

ENDPAPERS

Front: Aboriginal stockmen's camp, Wave Hill Station, Northern Territory

Rear: The illegal gambling game of two-up (tossing two pennies), photographed near derelict goldmines outside Kalgoorlie, Western Australia
(*Both courtesy of Axel Poignant Archive*)

Sources of Illustrations

Plates 1, 2, 3, 4, 5, 6, 9, 10, 13, 15, 17, 19, 21, 22, 23, 24, 25, 26, 27, 28, 29, 31, 32: Promotion Australia; 3: Government of Western Australia; 7, 8, 11, 14, 16, 20, 30: Wesley Stacey; 12: Narelle Perroux; 18: Sydney Hilton International Hotel.

Melville Is.

DARWIN

Ja█

Katherine

Wyndham

Derby

Broome

Port Hedland

Great Sandy Desert

One

Highway

NORTHE█

Macdo█

Tropic of
Capricorn

Gibson Desert

Mt Olga ▲ ▲ U█

(Ayers R█

WESTERN AUSTRALIA

SOUTH
AUSTRA█

Geraldton

Cervantes

Nullarbor Plain

Eucla█

Norseman

Fremantle ● PERTH

Cocklebiddy
Cave

Str█

Denmark Albany

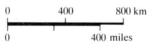

0   400   800 km
├──────────┼────────────┤

0   400 miles

─────── Road route mentioned in text

∼∼∼∼∼∼ Rivers mentioned in text

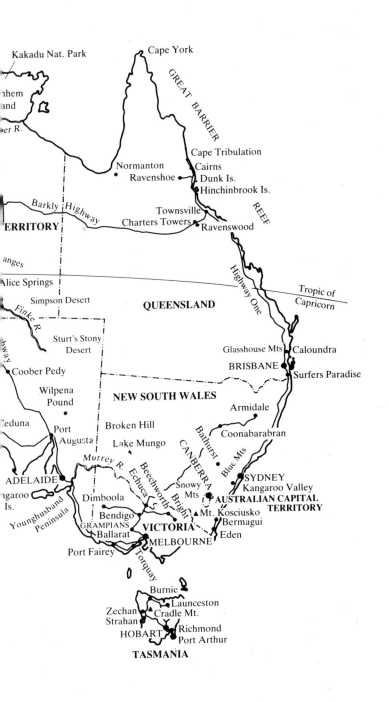

INTRODUCTION

When I was a child in England during the Second World War we lived at Stroud in Gloucestershire. This small Cotswold town was not a target for the Germans, of course, but Swansea was. Homebound enemy bombers, being harassed by RAF fighters, off-loaded their remaining bombs to gain maximum height (their chief defensive manoeuvre) and speed. These were the bombs which occasionally, randomly and quite unmaliciously, fell our way.

When the sirens sounded, my widowed mother marshalled us into a team, my elder brother and sister and myself, to wheel the settee across the floor till the back rested against the keyboard of our majestic upright piano (of German make), forming a tunnel which might safely house us when the roof fell in. Quite reasonably supposing we might be terrified – which we were, though I also recall it as a lively relief from dull routines – my mother sought to distract us by bringing out a box of special photographs. These pictures, kept in a Players 100 tin were taken during her adolescence when the family still lived at Kangaroo Valley, New South Wales.

We pored over the sepia images by torchlight, each print being passed from hand to hand, accompanied by the torch. As the youngest I was habitually last in line, a precious privilege for a lingerer. So these scenes became a private world. The sporadic arrival of food parcels from remote persons referred to as Aunty This or Uncle That confirmed the enticement of Australia, my secret land; not only for the tinned pineapple and butter or the melon and lemon jam, but for the utterly unBritish manner of stitching the boxes in beautifully fitted calico covers.

The photographs showed our grandparents and their young family in the Australian bush, pursuing a fulltime occupation of picnicking, shooting wildlife, and preserving their civilised decorum even though – or perhaps especially because – no one was there to see. In one snap my grandfather stood with smoking rifle over the corpse of a large black snake ('This was a surprise visitor at home in Kangaroo Valley,' my mother explained); in another, our grandmother held out her arms toward the camera with what appeared to be a length of cord draped over them ('An earthworm at Kangaroo Valley') six feet long! In another my mother herself, as a spritely young woman, stood beside a miniature dolomite almost twice her height and smiled out at me from a glazed print with a crack across it where somebody had accidentally bent the corner, even as her older self smiled in the ghastly edges of torchlight against the warplanes' lofty thunder. ('That's an anthill.') How could she be leaning there, smiling, I marvelled, when the blasted thing must be full of giant ants? Under canopies of colossal treeferns, astonishing to a lad convinced that the ordained height for a fern is up to one's thigh or waist at most, ladies in crisp blouses and long skirts sat around blankets spread on the ground, interrupted while arranging the starched tablecloths with profligate piles of food. There were never any houses in these pictures, let alone towns. Nor were there any open prospects. No one outside the immediate family circle ever intruded upon them. Into that enclosed jungle of monstrous overgrowths and intimate occasions I ventured in imagination. I possessed it. This was my land, which one day I would claim.

When I was thirteen we migrated to Brisbane. For our mother the journey in 1949 marked a permanent return; for us a first arrival. I can't speak on behalf of the others; but for myself, with my store of images, I knew exactly what to expect. Small wonder, then, that I have perhaps never got over my amazement at Australia as I found it to be.

We disembarked at Sydney to be met by chill blustery weather and seemingly endless bureaucratic delays through customs. The overnight train journey north to Brisbane, sitting up for the entire fifteen hours, only to stagger out into hot sunshine and steamy humidity, completed our sense of alienation. The tedium and brutality of the life I was about to live at boarding school, followed by a stiff dose of subtropical suburbia, as well as several stints drudging as a junior clerk and delivery boy in the city completed the picture. On top of all this, I was mocked and reviled for being a pommie (an accusation now grown mercifully rarer) every time I opened my mouth and let out my BBC accent.

Eight years passed before I recaptured any magic at all in the word *Australia*.

Right in the centre of this flattest, driest and most ancient of continents, there is a single rock. Over a thousand feet high and more than seven and a half miles around the base, Ayer's Rock – Uluru to the Aborigines – is the world's largest monolith. At dawn it sits like a rough ruby on the brown plain, while at midday it is an orange-coloured whale floating among orange waves of sand. In the evening it glows gold. And then, as the earth turns, a smoky amethyst tide creeps up to envelop it, a shadow rising like a memory of water from the desert which was a seabed many millions of years ago.

I first climbed the rock in 1957 when there was not even a road there. My bushwalker companions and I stood on the top in the most absolute, cosmic silence imaginable. Indeed, the mystical power of that experience reached beyond imagining, beyond any scale the mind had previously learned. A stillness and total solitariness filled me with ecstasy. I have travelled the world since but I have never found anything like it again. Nor is this possible now at Uluru itself. Thanks to the tourist industry's all-consuming obsession with modern comforts, a chain has been strung the whole way up one slope for people to catch hold of and help haul themselves to the top; there are tourist facilities, helicopters, frequent coaches, light aircraft; and, finally, a complete luxury resort nestling among the dunes where one can float on an air mattress in the swimming-pool sipping a strawberry daiquiri and getting a good view of the rock from the coolest, most seductive of prospects. Yulara Tourist Resort is beautifully designed and appointed and truly luxurious. But despite the fact that it lies discreetly low against the land, the effect is devastating. Of course in one sense Uluru remains bigger than anything man can do to it. The first glimpse still takes one's breath away, the view from the top is still awesome – but the untouched purity of the place as it was so little time ago has been violated. The spiritual intensity which had been such that one felt the rock as a vast presence, a sentient organism, depended upon the entire panorama remaining virginal. This is gone and will not be felt again, at least during our lifetime.

The history of Uluru raises several issues essential to understanding the whole country, even the cities with their millions of suburbanites.

Nowhere on earth is the land more essential in determining the character of the community, both black and white. The British invasion began in 1788 at Sydney. Other convict-built ports were set up during the following half-century and settlements were established at various isolated points around the coast, at Hobart, Perth, Melbourne, and Brisbane. Then Adelaide was founded as a free man's enterprise. Each town became the administrative centre for a colony. Boundary lines were drawn by the compass, north/south and east/west, in all but a few cases regardless of the terrain and in absolutely all cases regardless of the traditional owners. This dividing of the land told its own story about British attitudes to the place, which was regarded purely as real-estate from which would be extracted whatever might be practically converted to wealth for the Empire. Though the Empire has disintegrated, the attitude is still, lamentably, much the same. As a consequence of this arbitrary carving up of the cake, we still have an extraordinarily clumsy system of government, with separate state legislature as well as a federal parliament in Canberra. A continuing internecine wrangle is still being waged over just about every area of income and expenditure – not to mention issues of principle.

In October 1985 the Australian government put into effect its controversial plan of handing over the title of Ayer's Rock to an Aboriginal trust comprising sixteen members. This trust then leased Uluru back to the government as a national park. The outcry was immediate. The Northern Territory government launched a $200,000 protest campaign in the press and a former Chief Minister of the Territory (where the rock is situated) declared it to be 'a sell-out of the Australian nation'. The ferocity, the pain and, one might almost say, the jealousy of these diatribes revealed how fragile our seeming security is. We may claim to own the land, since arriving here in 1788, but plainly there is still a good deal of touchiness and guilt underlying that ownership. The handover of Uluru was, after all, little more than a gesture, having been empowered by a special act of parliament which may be revoked at any time.

The Aborigines themselves were not deceived. When the time came for the official ceremony they addressed a note to Bob Hawke, the Prime Minister, Clyde Holding, the Aboriginal Affairs Minister, and Sir Ninian Steven, the Governor-General, saying: 'Dear Bob, Clyde and Sir Ninian,

Have gone bush for law business and celebration. Please put "title papers" under the door of our office. Thank you. The Mutitjulu Community (on behalf of the traditional owners).'

One hundred thousand tourists visit Uluru each year and it is expected that this figure will double within five years. They come to see the rock, but also to experience its 'Aboriginality'. They want to feel something of the forty thousand years' accumulation of religious ceremonials, they also want to see some sample natives, preferably naked and painted, and ideally in the middle of a corroboree, chanting, stamping and dancing all night round a campfire. The local people, understandably, resent being stared at. They resent having their settlement invaded by photographers who behave as if nobody but themselves needs privacy and who persist in such behaviour because this is what they paid for, and they feel it is their right.

Central Australia is perhaps the one place on the map where visitors and the land's original inhabitants are almost bound to come face to face, with relatively little buffering by white Australians. Nowhere else can one encounter so clearly the sense of a continuing invasion. Even under the space-age canopies of Yulara Tourist Resort, the sunburnt visitor floating in the pool cannot help but sense the enormity and strangeness of the land. Marooned and left here to survive, he would be about as much at home as on the moon.

I shall begin our journey through Australia where the first British arrivals began theirs, at Sydney. Actually, Captain Cook missed the magnificent harbour, though it was precisely what he was looking for. What he did discover was nearby Botany Bay, and this was where they waded ashore – 1030 persons, comprising the Governor, Arthur Phillip, his staff of nine, as well as a surveyor-general, a surgeon and four assistants, a chaplain and his wife and two servants, 211 marines, twenty-seven wives and nineteen children of marines, and 736 convicts with seventeen children. They brought with them supplies of flour, rice, salted beef and pork, dried peas and butter, a miscellaneous mob of sheep, hogs, goats, puppies, turkeys, geese, ducks, chickens, pigeons and cats, one bull, one bull-calf, seven cows, one stallion, three mares and three colts.

If we imagine ourselves, by contrast, as arriving with a suitcase, some hand baggage and a camera, this is a convenient ready image for how far Sydney has come since the days of being the furthest outpost of imperial mercantile opportunism. The commonest error of judgment a British visitor can make is to forget those intervening years and treat Australians possessively, with affectionate condescension, with a metaphorical pat on the head, as if to say, 'Really, you are "ours" already, of course.' And to the alert visitor, the differences will soon appear every bit as striking as the similarities.

1   *Bliss on the Beach*

SYDNEY ~ NEW SOUTH WALES

Although there is no doubt in my mind that the ideal approach to Sydney is by sea, with a triumphal progress up the harbour in an ocean liner, the more usual way is by air. And this, too, has a special quality of unreality. If you come in across the Pacific, Sydney does indeed drift below like one possible version of paradise. From the air, the ugly details are too diminished to be seen. The overall impression is of sun-drenched suburbs spreading inland from beaches where waves cream along white sand and round the indented shore-line of countless scooped-out coves, over knobbly headlands and following branched river-courses, everywhere in contact with glittering water, the harbour reaching inland with its scores of liquid fingers. In short, the whole vista holds together as a marvellously integrated city culminating in an impressive cluster of office towers marching down to Sydney Cove itself.

This exciting vision is not easy to recapture once you are on the ground and besieged by a conflicting clamour of advertising hoardings, ugly shopfronts, miles of grubby streets, miscellaneous small factories and shops. But that paradisal city can still, occasionally, be experienced. Every so often, in a glimpse of harbour, a jigsaw of Paddington's charming terrace-houses, a flutter of plane-tree leaves in Martin Place, a ferry gliding towards a tiny landing-stage, it is there and you know that, to the people who live here, the city has a special character. Knowledge of this glamour penetrates even to the farthest corner of those endless miles of depressing suburbs which almost reach the Blue Mountains themselves in the west.

Writing in the *Tatler* the English novelist Angela Carter said: 'Sydney is as beautiful a city as you can imagine. It's coming up for its moment ... it's still a secret that Australia likes to keep. It's one of the five most beautiful cities in the world. The sea is everyone's backyard. It's magical because it is only just happening ... clearly perched on the edge of this enormous ocean.' Though we may warm to such enthusiasm for our oldest city, I'm sure most Australians would object strenuously to the notion that we have been trying to keep it a secret. On the contrary, we've been flaunting it, complete with nude bodies on Bondi beach, glossy advertisements of yachts nodding like exotic lilies over the glittering harbour, we've been shouting ourselves hoarse, offering to sell to the highest bidder if only someone out there will believe us. Sydney *is* a beautiful city, but it is also a vulgar city in many ways, and a city of sprawling suburbs few of which enjoy more than a dream of the ocean as a backyard and may indeed be an hour's agonising drive away, through cluttered streets and wilfully red traffic-lights.

The phrase that most strikes home is Angela Carter's observation that Sydney is 'magical because it is only just happening'. Like most Australian cities, Sydney is a perpetual worksite, buildings being demolished and vast office towers going up on all sides, the streets being excavated for a new electric rail system here or a harbour tunnel there. Of course, this is a phenomenon common in many parts of the world but what makes it worth remarking upon here is the scale at which it is happening in relation to the settled aspects of the city. In fact, there seems to be no permanent city at all, no heart to the place which remains constant while changes go on around it. What remains constant is the water. Even for those who do not enjoy the privilege of looking on it, Sydney

10

is a water city. The magnificent harbour, lying like a broad river estuary, is broken into scores of little sandy coves separated by rocky headlands. This is not one of those vast expanses of sheltered water so wide that buildings on the opposite shore are seen only like a different city and even tall towers dwindle to toy-size. At all points, the harbour gives the impression of holding its waterfront suburbs in contact with one another rather than separating them. Huge as its volume is, the waterway is so shaped that it never loses intimacy or the sense of variety in detail.

To travel on the ferries is by far the best way of appreciating Sydney. Even just coming from the north-westerly suburbs, for example, you may savour the full experience.

You set out across the inner reaches of the harbour, among other large ferries and sundry light craft; sailing boats nod past and people wave. Leaving the bosky shores of Hunters Hill or Greenwich, looking back at expensive houses nestling among luxuriant gardens, the ferry arrives at Long Nose Point and then Balmain where the housing is denser, very largely comprising terraced dwellings, regarded until recent years as a working-class district, cheerful in character but low on the scale of living standards. You sweep past the dockyards at Johnston's Bay and Darling Harbour, dominated by the Port Authority tower, where container ships and freighters fly the flags of maritime nations from all round the world, on past the warehouses of Walsh Bay (now refurbished as restaurants and a theatre), to the only truly awesome structures in Australia: the bridge and the opera house. The ferry steams right under the Sydney Harbour Bridge, so one may look up among the web of steel struts and watch commuter trains shuttling along on the western side. And then, like passing through a gateway, the boat swings round the point straight towards the Opera House. At whatever time of day you travel and whatever the season,

11

whether the great white pottery sails are gleaming like polished eggshell in the soft dawn, or sparkling and hard-edged at midday in summer, or lambently floodlit at night, whether it is seen through veils of lashing rain or in a mysterious drift of autumn mist, or simply standing in bleak overcast weather gazing at its reflection in the still harbour, the Opera House is superb.

Yet the story of the building is not a happy tale. In January 1957 the Danish architect Jørn Utzon was announced the winner of an international competition (out of 233 entries from thirty-two countries) with his design and was sturdily (one might almost say, heroically) supported by the New South Wales state government of the day while he solved each structural problem as it arose. The idea was improvised, in a sense, and each solution broke new ground, from the geometry of the domes to the glaze of the covering tiles. The result promised to be stunning. Then the Labor government fell and an accountant-ridden administration took office, thanks to their appeal to the ocker vote. (An ocker – a very Australian word, this – is a self-professed larrikin, at best earthy and warm-hearted, at worst a coarse, narrow-minded, anti-intellectual bigot, not to put too fine a point on it.) The ockers were delighted at a firm stand being made against public expenditure on anything to do with the arts. Loudly protesting at the escalating cost of the building, the new government made Utzon's life impossible, with the result that in February 1966 he resigned with the job half-finished. The long-term tragedy for Australia is hard to estimate. A team of public servants went to work and other architects were engaged to complete the task. They managed creditably enough, but the bold masterstrokes of Utzon's solutions ceased abruptly. The interior stage tower was sold to Spain before it even left the German factory. The opera theatre was converted to a concert hall and the smaller concert hall forced to do duty, well beyond its capacity, for staging operas. But whatever its shortcomings, the building stands as a giant free-standing sculpture, jutting right out into the water, an enrichment to the life of every Sydneysider who sets eyes on it. And, despite the cafeteria-standard snacks served on the open-air concourse, even quarter of an hour sipping coffee there, watching the leisurely activity of the harbour, is an experience never to be forgotten.

Sad to relate, the Harbour Bridge is another case of a great structure marred by an architectural blunder. The famous steel 'coathanger' comprises the entire support for the bridge – called a suspended-deck arch. What, then, of the four granite pylons, a pair at each end, which dominate the design? They are purely ornamental and have no function in holding up the bridge. And unfortunately they *do* dominate. So that, instead of soaring up and reaching a visual climax at its peak, the arch appears anchored lumpishly to either shore. At the time it was built, in 1932, an exposed steel frame was thought ugly. The result of this whimsy is that what might have been a fine, free leap across a wide stretch of water appears rather pompous and earthbound.

The fate of such government building projects, which ought not to be plagued by the randomness and competitive ostentation of commercial architecture, will be seen as lamentably consistent when mention is made later on of the national capital, Canberra.

Even so, the bridge has this in common with the Opera House – spoiled though the concept was, the effect is still memorable in its own right.

Travelling from suburb to suburb, one is struck by how different they are, how self-contained in character, and village-like. This is largely a result of the extremely varied land forms. Sydney and Brisbane are alike in having hilly sites fragmented by gullies and waterways, which contrast strik-

13

ingly with Melbourne and Adelaide. This variety of land forms contributes equally to the city's charm, on one hand, and the impossible traffic conditions, on the other – traffic conditions much exacerbated by having only two bridges across the harbour to connect the huge spread of residential and business districts in the north and north-west with the even more huge spread of city and industrial suburbs to the south and south-west. The volume of traffic sweeps in along freeways, to come to a characteristic halt at the bottleneck of Sydney Harbour Bridge. But the frustrations do not end there: unless you take one of the freeways skirting the city centre, once you drive off the bridge, you find yourself undergoing another endurance test of the virtue of patience. You crawl through the narrow clogged streets of the old part of town, where the eccentric angles of intersections and dog-leg streets are surviving reminders of the irregular course of long-vanished creeks and of fords which ceased to have anything to ford well before the horse-and-buggy days were over. To anyone not in a hurry this irregularity is charming and full of character. It is the very antithesis of a planned city.

What, then, of the more recent planning at present being put into effect? The great project is Darling Harbour. This waterfront area, running parallel with the entire city centre, has become available for development since container ships made the old wharf facilities obsolete, and the virtual death of passenger shipping closed the terminals. The New South Wales state government is pouring vast resources into a scheme to build a complex of exhibition buildings, museums, markets, convention venues and restaurants there. Darling Harbour is to be connected to the city by a monorail shuttling once every two minutes and looping up through the centre of town. On paper the project looks light and airy, with the latest trend in flimsiness. Publicity brochures have been

14

produced at considerable expense to cajole the public into approving the scheme. But the reception has been lukewarm at best, and openly aggressive at worst. Already the pylons of the monorail clutter the narrow city streets and people don't like it. What they see is that much of the familiar Sydney is being made a backyard for the waterfront extravagances at Darling Harbour. This project may not be unreasonable, but it has not yet begun to endear itself to the working Sydneysider. The publicity asserts that the development will 'give the centre back to the people', but, with its emphasis on the international hotel/casino set, many believe it is simply another invasion of living space to provide luxuries for the rich.

The disused wharves have already been demolished and steel structures have begun to rise, ready to support concrete vaults and acres of flat roof suspended by cables from tall towers. In my view, it will be a major asset for Sydney, but nowhere near as alive as it might have been had the scheme escaped the monument syndrome, the gigantism of so much public planning. What is missing is housing. The whole thing is an embodiment of the Pleasure Principle, the assumption that you bring life to a place by filling it with a supermarket of diversions. The simple truth is that unless people actually live in an area, it will never come fully alive. During opening hours and in times of affluence, I'm sure it will be busy, with satisfied people reassuring one another that they are, in fact, having a great time. But after hours and in the inevitable periods of economic depression, my guess is that the area will be as sparsely populated as that other folly of public posturing, Canberra. The scale of each building, like the scale of the various parks and gardens, is too grandiose. Huge areas of lawn become as forbidding as no greenery at all. The flat open spaces of the main park will, I expect, prove far less popular than the broken shapes of the Chinese Garden they

15

are setting round a pond. This, incidentally, is to be strategically placed (mock-pagoda and all) to lead out towards Dixon Street, the traditional Chinese area, which in recent times has been tarted up, with gaudy lanterns and Disneyland artificiality, as a lure for tourists.

Sydney's Chinatown, smaller and more limited than the one in San Francisco, nevertheless still offers good shopping and a selection of restaurants: from westernised places with waiters in black ties to the Hingara's simple kitchen tables and chairs and what seems to be a perpetual crowd of Chinese customers, where the food is excellent and the servings generous. At Chinese New Year (usually in the first weeks of February) some minor but colourful rituals can be watched in the district, including a ceremony of blessing shops, when a paper dragon undulates along the pavements gobbling up offerings of sweets which the shopkeepers hang at first-floor level for it to reach and young men blow strident reed instruments while others bang gongs and drums.

The Vietnamese community is also very strong, centred on the suburb of Cabramatta. But there is no sense in which you could say this has become a ghetto. They fit into the Australian mainstream remarkably successfully. This integration of immigrant minorities is perhaps less clearly seen at the beach than elsewhere – only because the addiction to leisure in the sun hasn't taken over their lives. But they're getting there. More and more are to be seen lounging on the sand with every appearance of having nothing better to do because there *is* nothing better to do. And that's a style we recognise as belonging.

Going to the beach is not just a matter of an annual holiday, but an important factor in everyday life.

Mere mention of the beach raises a host of issues, starting with the historical foundation of the nation as it is known today.

16

The accusation is heard frequently that Australians talk a great deal about being Australian. I call this an accusation because every time I have come across it, the tone has been disapproving or even mocking. But what could be more exciting and fascinating than to help fashion a new national consciousness? *Of course* we talk with endless enthusiasm about what is or is not 'Australian' – because we are trying to define it for ourselves. This is our passion, our vocation, our privilege. The components which go into the making of the national mores are as ancient as anywhere in the world: from the undoubted – one might say aristocratic – lineage of Aboriginal culture, to the disparate roots of the white community reaching back to Ireland and Scotland, to England, Italy, Germany, to the civilisations of old Vikings and ancient Greeks, through Chinese immigrants to the manners and philosophy of remote dynasties, and through Vietnamese refugees to the Mongolian ancestors of those farmers who settled along the banks of the Red River. The list could be endless. The mix is a new one, analagous to the creation a hundred years ago of a fairly settled Americanism.

It is a mistake to use a phrase such as 'a young country', because both the place and the social elements being melded here are already immemorial. The freshness comes of the unique combination being formed, the contribution of chance, that great unknown factor of whether the experiment will be a success or a disaster. And the whole process is given a refreshing quality by the fact that we are free from the yardstick of suffering. In Europe (and possibly in Asia too) there is an underlying morality of pain: that virtue only comes of suffering. Even that knowledge of the world just comes of suffering also. We do not accept this. We believe there are other ways to goodness and sophistication. And in this respect we have something deeply in common with Americans: we are, unashamedly, a pleasure-centred society. This places us very firmly in the mainstream of Pacific cultures.

It is not, then, so surprising that sport plays a vital part in the nation's psyche – sport, that is, as an extension of pleasure. This is not, I think, quite like the European passion for sport, where football or athletics have become more akin to formalised war-play than games for the sheer sake of exuberance. It is a fine line I am drawing. Distinctions are not always clear; and there is no such thing as homogeneity in Europe any more than here. All I am able to do is to sketch general guidelines, to put this forward as a possible description of the contrast in attitudes a visitor might find. And I believe it is a help to understand that we do not feel we have missed the 'real' experience of the world for never having suffered a war since the days when we ourselves invaded the place. Nor is our dedication to sport necessarily mindless.

The most popular sport is fishing: from the contemplative pleasures of throwing in a line off the beach or the rocks, to the alert artfulness of angling for trout, to the brute thrills of big-game marlin fishing. Each year Australians spend some $1125 million on boats and equipment, boat-trailers, rods and tackle and the manifold accoutrements of the sport. Part of the special magic of fishing is – once more – the obsession with water.

In my own mind, I connect this with the significance of beaches and with the keen interest in sailing as well. Sailing, expensive in relation to other sports, is popular nonetheless; as a glimpse of Saturday afternoon on the harbour, or Pittwater, or the Derwent River in Hobart, Port Phillip in Melbourne, the Swan River in Perth, or even Canberra's Lake Burley Griffin will show. There may be more to this love of watersports than casual hedonism, or relief from a hot climate.

Right at the outset, people understood that in this dry

18

continent, water, the key to survival, could not be taken for granted. In the interior a spring was precious, a river a miracle. Even along the fertile coast water needed to be conserved. And then, of course, the early settlements were all ports. To this day, Australians are predominantly coastal; eighty per cent of the people live along the seaboard. The establishment of port facilities for the empire was the whole idea of claiming *Terra Australis* (which means simply the 'south land') in the first instance. So, while the Aborigines survived by time-honoured skills at knowing where water was to be found, white communities huddled on the cliff-edge of a vast and threateningly empty hinterland, facing the sea as if this were a comfort in itself. In short, they looked outward: their supplies, their contact with the old world, their only escape from a life of servitude here, was via ships. This is not so much a tradition as an ingrown island mentality. Despite the instant global contact of modern telecommunications, despite the frequency and comfort of flying abroad on any of the dozen or so airlines running international services to and from Australia each day, even despite the continental vastness of the land itself, we are still perhaps essentially islanders.

There are splendid surfing beaches in all states (Western Australia and Queensland being especially proud of theirs), but New South Wales must take the palm as the beach state. Unlike the Queensland coastline, most of which is sheltered from open surf by the Great Barrier Reef, or Western Australia with its fewer and scattered resorts, the entire New South Wales coast, 1100 kilometres long, comprises sandy beaches.

To postulate any sort of social psychology based on our beach culture is chancy, but such a risk does seem called for, precisely because the beach is accepted as a significant factor in the general lifestyle. No sight in Australia looks quite so incongruous, as newly arrived foreigners, fully dressed in

19

shoes and suits and ties, stockings and dresses and handbags, walking on the sand: people for whom the beach is an unfamiliar environment.

Young and old alike, we come into our inheritance at the beach. This is not just the vigorous matter of riding the surf or swimming, nor even just hedonism while toasting one's body in the sun(though these are important elements). At the risk of sounding comic, it is something like a symbol of our liberation from the strictures of the old world. There is a sense in which we take off our clothes with the cheerful relief of people affirming by this simple gesture their birthright in being free as the elements. Whether we are ugly or beautiful, it makes no difference. The beach is our domain, where we make space our own: immersed in the limitless ocean or touched by the limitless sky. The transformation is visible anywhere. One look at the people on a beach, at their eyes, their posture, is enough. They are not simply there for a dip or a rare picnic, they are habitués renewing themselves by shedding their workaday lives.

Also embedded in this symbolism lies some element of the passion for equality. One cannot avoid meeting with it. The first thing Australians will ask is your name – and they mean your first name. Everyone is on first-name terms. If you wish to have your say, even on foreign policy, you can ring the relevant Minister in Canberra and the chances are he or she, if free, will speak to you. You introduce yourself and before you know where you are, you're being called by your first name and you're calling him Bill, or her Susan. It is our pride that this familiarity does not impair the dignity of office, nor does it deceive people into forgetting who has power and who has not. It is an expression of origins, perhaps. We began on the bottom rung. The nation grew from the sweat of convicts, social outcasts. Just as the Rats of Tobruk pride themselves on being called rats, so we pride ourselves

1 Almost resembling a set from some Steven Spielberg film, Sydney Opera House is lit up spectacularly by fireworks, jazz bands and a flotilla of small boats in the harbour to herald a New Year

2 Frozen music echoes off the sheer sandstone cliffs of The Escarpment on the Arnhem Land plateau, Northern Territory

3 Wave Rock, a cresting-wave formation near Hyden, Western Australia

4 Surfers' Paradise on the Gold Coast, a built-up resort area in Queensland

on a past for which we owe thanks to no one. The beach, too, is a leveller. Once stripped and spreadeagled in the sun, how can anyone tell who drove there in the BMW parked outside the fish-and-chip shop and who came by bus?

To miss going to the beach – and I do not mean simply viewing it, the way we might visit a zoo – is like going to Hong Kong and refusing to do any shopping. The beaches are physically stimulating and sociologically fascinating.

When departing from Sydney, I would advise anyone who arrived without flying across the country's inland areas, to be sure to fly out that way. You should insist on a window seat and a daylight schedule. As the city slips away beneath you, as a stippled sea of red roofs among tree-filled gardens sheared off by the blue and white edges of the coast, you fly out across the most extraordinary, map-like landscape, a grand expanse of space, across the muted colours and wrinkled landforms of the mysterious outback.

The early British colonists found even the trees unfamiliar in form, with a peculiar range of greens: sometimes grey-green, sometimes brownish, sometimes almost silvery. The animals were already a sensation. The word *kangaroo* had a place in just about any language with a claim to sophistication. The parrots and budgerigars were exported with merciless enthusiasm and much prized by their purchasers for brilliant plumage and teachability in the matter of 'talking'. There was even a bird with a maniac laugh, the kookaburra, commonly referred to as a 'laughing jackass', which few people realised was a species of giant kingfisher.

Those first immigrants and convicts, whether joyful or grumbling, set about converting the bush to a likeness of 'home'. They brought demoniac energy to this mission, felling forests, fencing tracts of country, ploughing, planting, and herding the beasts they brought with them. They built houses and grew possessive about the wilderness they had

21

come to live in, even if only temporarily. And it should be pointed out that many had no intention of staying longer than it would take to amass a fortune they could spend more enviably in Britain.

Explorers returned with tales of sandy deserts, deserts of rounded stones, salt lakes filled with shimmering mirages, tropical jungles and snow-clad mountains. Not only did they open the way for the insatiable settlers to spread out from their original landing points, but they began furnishing the Australian imagination with a heroic identity.

The new arrivals fell into two camps: those who found the bush intolerably drab, couldn't see any wildflowers (though the ground might be dotted with them throughout the year) and were deaf to the birdsong around them because it did not fit into recognised patterns; and those who felt invigorated by the open spaces, the challenge of so much for which they had no names as yet.

The country still demands an ability to adjust to the unfamiliar. Even the air itself is different. And this is not just a fanciful description of the quality of light. The Blue Mountains do indeed stand blue on the horizon as you approach them, not from any peculiarity of their own, but because of the forest at the foot of the range. The atmosphere, especially on a hot summer day, is saturated with particles of eucalyptus oil given off by the leaves. This phenomenon is known scientifically as Rayleigh Scattering and causes the blue end of the spectrum to be refracted more intensely. Hence the effect.

Eucalyptus trees are common enough in many parts of the world now. But here, in their native environment, they mass very differently from the carefully planted samples one sees in Valencia or Agra. Also there are more than four hundred varieties, many of which flower as spectacularly as chestnut trees. Huge areas might strike the visitor as panoramas of unbroken, homogenous treetops, bewildering in their extent and consistency, like those dark trackless forests of fairy-tales where it is impossible to tell which direction is which, or find one's way home. In fact, when you venture into these forests, the chances are they will not have that feel at all.

Most beautiful is the spotted-gum (*eucalyptus maculata*). To walk among these lofty trees with their slender, smooth, pale trunks, branchless for perhaps sixty feet right up to the crown of leaves, is like being in the luminous spaces of a columned cathedral. The light changes with the seasons as the trees shed their bark: from dove grey in spring through to a summer cream and then green in autumn, mottling as winter comes on. The open forest, its floor tufted with macrozamia palms – among the oldest living things on earth – is majestic and airy. The south coast of New South Wales is especially rich in this kind of forest, which, unlike the truly spooky antarctic beech forests of Tasmania, is easy to get to. Forestry Commission roads, though little more than tracks, usually provide good all-weather access quite usable by the ordinary family car.

I always urge visitors to go out of the cities and see something of life on the land. In Australia it is often the style of living, the resourcefulness, even the crazy unlikelihood of how people manage, which is interesting, rather than the standard 'sights'.

I recall one old chap giving me a lift once in his little truck. On an isolated dirt track we broke down.

'Let me see, now,' he said, and I could have sworn he was pleased as he opened the bonnet and peered inside. 'Scout around for some wire, mate,' he said, 'we don't need much but it has to be tie-wire, fencing-wire's no good. I need a few other bits and pieces but I'm sure to find a wreck somewhere hereabouts.'

I thought this was rather a tall order as I watched him

23

walk off into the bush. But, sure enough, within quarter of an hour he was back, whistling cheerfully. And I had found just the thing, too. So he got to work with his pliers and promised me we'd be on the track in next to no time. A couple of hours later we were able to creep cautiously the twenty kilometres to the nearest service station. There the old man was in his element explaining the problem, and how he had worked out a temporary solution, while a 'bush mechanic' (a common phrase for a man who often makes his living fixing vehicles but has no trade certificate) rigged up a slightly more durable makeshift version of road-worthiness to get us home.

Often enough it is the things that go wrong which are the most interesting. And the penalty of being in a rush and perpetually worried about your schedule is that you are not leaving room for time and chance to show you a way into the real life and charm of the people. I suppose this is the same anywhere. But city habits do tend to be the traveller's worst enemy. And in Australia the contrast between the city and the country is indeed extreme.

Even hitchhikers frequently fall into this error. I very frequently pick up youth hostellers on the Prince's Highway, which links Sydney and Melbourne, and I know that all along this route there are fascinating backroads and beautiful beaches. Many times, I have offered to stop and point the direction to a particularly delightful spot in easy reach. Every single one of these young people, male and female, Australian and foreign, has said something like: 'Thank you but I want to reach Melbourne by tonight,' or Sydney, or, in one far-fetched case, 'Cairns by the day after tomorrow.'

Leaving Sydney, you either choose one of the coastal routes, or you set out westwards for the Blue Mountains.

Both south and north of Sydney lie coalmining districts which have been worked for well over a century. The northern ones are centred on Newcastle (where else?) and the southern ones on Wollongong. It was to the small mining town of Thirroul on the south coast that D. H. Lawrence came in May 1922 when he rented a bungalow called Wyewurk and wrote his Australian novel, *Kangaroo* (1923), about a fictional fascist leader nicknamed 'Kangaroo'. Inland of Wollongong lies the beautiful Kangaroo Valley, named in this case for the animal itself. One approaches it either through the Macquarie Pass or across Cambewarra Mountain. Cambewarra is by far the better route because it brings you right to the foot of Kangaroo Valley, opening out to a delightful prospect of fertile fields and fruit trees, backed by lofty curtains of cliff-faces, down which flow several waterfalls. After good rains when there is plenty of water in the catchment area, the Fitzroy Falls look particularly magnificent, dropping 700 feet in two stages and ending in cascades at the bottom.

Although one may still find treeferns and, very occasionally, tall ant-hills, there is very little today in common with the magical, rather threatening world of my mother's old photographs. Perhaps the most haunting experience is to wander through the Wombeyan limestone caves. But, fine as they are, they are outdone by the state's most famous examples at Jenolan in the Blue Mountains, sixty kilometres further north. And the Blue Mountains deserve special mention anyway.

When my wife and I decided to move out to the country in 1972, we began our search in the Blue Mountains. It was an obvious choice, a mere hour by train from Sydney, having excellent bus services also, shopping centres and entertainment, plus splendid scenery and a community of people with a special brand of hospitality. Although, in the end, we did not buy the house for which we had begun negotiating, we did enjoy the bonus of frequent journeys to Mount

25

Victoria and getting to know the area. In the sixteen years since, there have been marked changes. The Blue Mountains resorts have benefited from something of a renaissance. Accommodation and services are far more sophisticated, and several quality restaurants have opened. The Cleopatra in Blackheath, standing back from the road in a fastidiously kept cottage garden, is a pretty Victorian house, adapted to accommodate ten guests; the restaurant serves very good French country cooking from Friday to Sunday. The surroundings, the fittings and ambiance of the place all make for an enjoyable experience. The cook, Dany Chouet, is French herself and justly proud of what she has achieved.

For contrast, we also tried the Paragon. Right in the centre of Katoomba, the main town of the Blue Mountains, the Paragon is a curious mixture of ugly glazed tiles and pretentious expensive foibles and fittings. But you need have no doubts about the chocolates made on the premises in ancient pans and cooled on a marble slab – *delicious* – or the peculiar charm of surroundings scarcely changed since 1916, when the café was built. There's heaps of Italian bric-à-brac, chandeliers and whatnot, amongst which one can enjoy a hearty roast lunch or simply sip the kind of soda I remember having as a child: drawn from an ornate soda fountain and tasting all the better for that. The Paragon is one of the two most famous establishments in the area. The other is the Hydro-Majestic Hotel in nearby Medlow Bath.

One quite commonly comes across people of a certain age who will wax eloquent about their memories of the Hydro-Majestic, dinners in the gilded dining room, balls in the ballroom, the rustle of taffeta, whirling figures, the men's black coat-tails flying, white bow ties and collars tight round red necks, diamonds twinkling and the odour of good times seeping right down through the years. But go there today, and the visitor would see very little of this in the lumpish and graceless building. Only its position on the edge of a cliff overlooking the magnificent Megalong Valley offers anything really special; the best room being the public bar, which is ironic because the original hotel was a spa, people went there for water: to bathe, wallow, be sprayed by and imbibe the natural mineral waters. Alcohol was strictly forbidden in those days.

For the tourist, curious to sample relics of Edwardian Australia, the Hydro-Majestic is fine. But those who crave real luxury might do better to book at the Fairmont Resort in Leura, developed at lavish expense from the ideal of an English manor house. But hold your breath when you get your bill.

The people who live in these little Blue Mountains towns seem to exist in a time warp of their own, hard to tie down, but somewhere between 1945 and 1960, a leisurely time tolerant of eccentricity and, though bathed in a gentle optimism for the future, not much wishing to hurry it along. Viewed from a distance, the mountains themselves are blue indeed and very beautiful. From close up, they are seen to be the scarp of a plateau. Huge faults and slippages of rock many thousands of years ago left walls of sheer cliff below which the scree slopes swoop down to wooded valleys. In sunlight, the mountains show wonderful warm colours, browns and ochres, which rain stains purple. Visitors to Sydney, even if restricted by a tight schedule and having only a few days, would be well advised to set aside at least one of them for a trip to the mountains.

An added attraction, as I began by saying, is to be found at Jenolan Caves. Playing straight into the hands of the last century's buccaneer romanticism, the caves were discovered by police searching for an elusive bushranger called McKeown. They were first known as McKeown's caves. Jenolan came later, being thought to be the native name for one of the mountains in the district and therefore more respectable as well as more appropriate. In 1866 one of the earliest government reserves, $6\frac{1}{4}$ square miles of land, was set aside around the entrance and an official 'Keeper of the Caves' appointed to take care of this extensive and magnificent show of stalactite and stalagmite formations. The stairways and electric lighting were put in last century, so the effect is dim and dusty, rather than too glaringly Disneyland.

A visit may be made all the more pleasant by staying at the modest Caves Guest House right outside.

A little farther inland, between Hartley and Lithgow, the country is pretty, if a little conventional, with green fields and cows, men on tractors, rocks and streams, offering the pleasure of long walks and good hearty meals at night. Hartley was once a staging post en route from Sydney to Bathurst, where Cobb & Co coaches changed horses and the hostelry did a roaring trade. Now it is a shadow of its former self, mouldering quietly in the valley, administered by the National Parks and Wildlife Service and visited only by sightseers. The convict-built court-house is one of the few early colonial buildings still in its original condition. Other buildings of interest are St Bernard's Church and Presbytery, several pleasant old hotels and cottages and the Post Office. The atmosphere is nostalgic and one is reminded of how small these outposts were, and how vast the surrounding ranges and forests.

There is now a widespread interest in colonial buildings and their uses, so they are being preserved and restored all over the country; the National Trust owns and manages a great many of them and is the best source of information about where they are to be found. Personally, I find most of the handsome residences (such as Sydney's Elizabeth Bay House and Melbourne's Como) rather impersonal and less interesting than outlying examples such as Saumarez at Armidale. This family house of some fourteen rooms plus servants' quarters, instead of being filled by the National Trust with beautiful old furniture far better than anything seen there while it was lived in by the hardbitten non-conformist White family (related to the grandparents of novelist Patrick White – Australia's greatest non-Aboriginal artist, and Nobel Prize winner), remains exactly as it was – spartan, redolent of doctrinaire parsimony and parental repression, filled by hideous homely items which the family apparently looked after with an obsessive care not even treasures would have warranted. The bedroom furniture, selected from a mail-order catalogue, looks gimcrack even today. Far from being a cold museum of good taste, Saumarez is the pathetic mausoleum of a successful grazier's smallness of mind and stultified sensibilities. As such, it offers the powerful experience of a glimpse behind the scenes, the unguarded truth about people who, during their lifetimes, held criticism strictly at bay. There is not one item in the house worth looking at in terms of its own quality, yet the whole place offers insights into a very particular style of life and the tragedy of its success.

Leaving Saumarez and driving through the back country from Armidale, down the Oxley and Newell highways to Victoria, you travel for 300 kilometres across open country punctuated now and again by rugged rocky outcrops, then into the feathery shade of close-growing pilliga scrub. Pilliga looks like a small, native pine. It forms a very light and reduced version of a European pine forest. Out once more on the vast western plains, the horizon lies far away and flat under the huge sky. To the south rises the star attraction of the area, a small mountain cluster, odd volcanic remains, called the Warrumbungles.

The peaks form fantastic nodules and tusks of rock jutting up out of tree-covered foothills. The colours of the bush, subtle as always, present delightful contrasts from silver-leafed shrubs seen against pink rock to white gumtree country. The white gums do not encourage undergrowth, so they stand round, rather small and old on a clear forest floor. Their trunks, streaked grey and cream, are as smooth as human skin. Frail yellowish leaves dangle to form a screen, infinitely delicate against the mountains across the valley: the ancient towers and bluffs of the range, wrinkled and rusty. The peaks themselves provide just about any kind of climbing one might desire. Some are simple grassy mounds perhaps two or three hundred feet high, others offer perilously worn overhanging cliffs for the expert. Wildlife abounds, with sulphur-crested cockatoos shrieking wildly, playful pink and grey galahs (also a cockatoo) swooping across the road, and scores of kangaroos browsing at their ease, too shy to be approached closely, but not nervous either, because this is a national park and they know from experience they are safe. The elegance of kangaroos in motion is as supreme as that of deer.

My favourite spot in the Warrumbungles is reached right at the outer edge of the range when approaching from Coonabarabran. This is known as Timor Rock. The vertical strata have been weatherworn so deeply that it looks as if it had been put together of ready-made parts. This warm brown rock, with its powdering of green lichen, has been aged to a thousand shapes like animal backs and human heads.

The best long-distance view of the range is from the Oxley Highway, thirty kilometres south of Coonabarabran. But don't leave the town without first calling at a little, privately run museum of local crystals, Crystal Kingdom. Despite its awful name, the samples are well displayed and stunningly beautiful. Among them are some fossils etched with remarkable clarity in the soft rock. The leaf fossils are the most colourful I have ever seen, slabs of white and pink stone scattered with leaves (perfect in every vein) of contrasting

shades, ochre and amber, some still with a greenish tinge –
a most astonishing and moving sight in a fossil – some
purplish brown on a putty-grey base.

Half a day's drive south you reach classic bushranger
country, the worked-out goldfield areas around Forbes,
Grenfell, Bathurst and down to Jerilderee. Australia's four
most famous bushrangers last century all committed their
highway robberies in this area – Captain Thunderbolt, Frank
Gardiner, Ned Kelly and Ben Hall.

Kelly and Hall (no family connection of mine) are among
the few true folk heroes we have. Hall, who was very handsome, had a sort of Dick Turpin charisma, despite his personal modesty and quiet disposition. He became an outlaw
as the result of harassment by troopers and Police Commissioner Sir Frederick Pottinger (a cold arrogant villain of
a figure). Hall returned to his farm one day to find it in
smoking ruins, the few cattle he owned slaughtered and his
wife run off with a policeman. He took to the hills and soon
made a name for himself by his daring escapades, his chivalry
to women – even while robbing them – and the fact that he
never killed anyone. His gang's greatest exploit was to hold
up the entire town of Canowindra, lock the police in their
own cells, take some leading citizens hostage in the pub and
'shout' the whole town to a three-day spree. I shall come
back to the term 'to shout' in a moment. But first I must make
clear how attractive this escapade was from an Australian
perspective. The audacity of giving the population a good
time is what strikes so strong a chord. This incident and Ned
Kelly's trial are the two highpoints of the romance (whether
true or false does not now matter) of these outlaws. Twenty
years after Hall had been betrayed, surrounded while asleep
and shot thirty-six times, Kelly faced trial in Melbourne in
1888. The passion and dignity of his speech were quite
extraordinary. Fearlessly he accused his judge and the corrupt

31

society he had set himself against. And even as the hangman slipped the noose round his neck he made history with the bravado of a joke, 'Such is life!'

As a footnote to the eccentricities of Australian colloquial usage, 'shouting' is an important one to know about. It is used in precisely the same way as 'stand' in to 'stand someone a drink'. Shouting is very common and accepted as one of the essential virtues. The man who is too mean to shout a round of drinks makes a fatally bad impression. A rogue is OK; so, to some degree, is a swindler; but a meanminded tightfisted anti-social bloke who won't even dip into his pocket when the round should plainly be on him, cuts himself off from the open welcome of people willing to be friendly.

A good way to enter Victoria is by this very road, reaching the boundary, the Murray River, as so many of the old stock routes did, at Echuca. For the present, I shall postpone this pleasure and look at another outback region of New South Wales.

The oldest human remains yet found in this country were unearthed in the flat lands of the state's far west. The site of the dig, Lake Mungo, is dead; there has been no water in it for 10,000 years. Those with energy may choose to walk the ten kilometres across the parched lake floor, but unless they have made arrangements to be picked up on the return journey, they had better plan to walk the whole round trip because there is seldom any traffic here. The objective, on the far bank, is a formation known locally as the Walls of China – perhaps because of their age, in addition to the fact that the approaches are made through grazing country where once Chinese shearers worked and built a splendid old shearing-shed on the bank of the lake. When you get there, the Walls of China crumble easily and great care needs to be taken to avoid damaging them. They are actually relics of a compacted sand dune, brittle though not yet as hard as rock, and worn away by ceaseless winds. They extend for some fifteen kilometres, like the rubble of towers and ruined bastions.

Lake Mungo formed part of the Lachlan River overflow system, once rich in food. Fish, shellfish, birds, and the snakes and marsupials which drank at the water's edge provided the tribespeople of so long ago with an ample diet. Our evidence is the midden (the 'kitchen waste') they left behind when the water dried up and they finally departed for more comfortable hunting grounds of their tribal territory. Modern carbon-dating techniques tell us this food was consumed some 38,000 years ago. It is the world's earliest known case of shellfish being included in the human diet.

When I arrived and drove to the ranger's hut standing beside that skeletal, ghostly shearing shed, I was in time to see a mini-busload of tourists returning from the archaeological site across the lake bed. As they got out, anticipating a cup of tea, one woman said: 'Is that all there is to it?' I remembered this, as I myself drove across the lake and wandered that wilderness of weather-worn sand towers, with not another human being in sight, my hair just about standing on end with the powerful sense that this was not like any other place on earth. So much more has been gouged out by wind and rain than remains, that the emptiness is palpable, pervaded by the sense of this loss. It is a place rich in ghosts.

As a warning against disappointment, I should point out that Lake Mungo, in common with many of the magic places of Australia, is not immediately spectacular to the eye. Its power eludes those who are there for a brief shot of prehistory. To absorb the feel of the place, you need to be alone (even if you travel with other people, you must assert your privacy once you arrive), receptive and willing to wait, to accept, and to wait some more. The rewards are beyond analysis.

33

At the archaeological dig two human skeletons have been found, one male and one female, both described in terms of the profession as 'extremely gracile', conjuring an image of slender agile people. Unquestionably this gives the site the mournful quality of a graveyard. One would need to be cursed with a brutish lack of imagination not to feel grief for what has been done in recent times to the descendants of these ancient people.

In 1887 A. W. Howitt, who lived in this very area, the man who had led the successful search party to find the ill-starred Burke and Wills expedition, collected and translated a song of the Woiworung tribe. The singer's name was Wenberi and the subject was his ancestors' and his own mortality:

> *We all go to the bones*
> *all of them shining white in the Dulur country.*
> *The noise of our father Bunjil*
> *rushing down singing inside this breast of mine.*

Howitt recalled how, listening to the old man, 'I was moved almost to tears.' He went on: 'In the tribes with which I have acquaintance I find it a common belief that the songs, using the word in its widest meaning, as including all kinds of Aboriginal poetry, are obtained by the bards from the spirits of the deceased, usually their relatives, during sleep in dreams.'

Lake Mungo, near Menindee, a long way off the beaten track, is strictly for those who already discover they have a feel for the mystery of the land.

2 *Mountains that Turn in their Sleep*

THE OUTBACK

Even Australians find it hard to comprehend the hugeness of their country. The best way to get an idea – short of attempting to walk across it with a couple of pack-mules or camels – is to fly in by daylight on a route that cuts across the continent from the north-west. This is a sight never to be forgotten, the sheer spread of land, so much of which is untouched, with no sign of habitation. The bizarre beauty of its calligraphic forms is unlike anywhere else on earth.

In statistical terms, Australia is 7,682,300 square kilometres; that is to say, some thirty-two times larger than the United Kingdom, or about one and a half times as big as the whole of Europe, excluding the Soviet Union. The Tropic of Capricorn passes across the northern part of the country, so most of the land mass enjoys a temperate climate of one kind or another (I shall be describing significant regional variations where appropriate), or else comes under the classification of arid desert. There are four main geographic regions: the western plateau, the interior lowlands, the eastern uplands, and the narrow coastal plain. The vast majority of Australia's 16 million people live on this coastal plain which runs right along the east coast, along part of the south coast, and re-emerges round the south-west corner of Western Australia. Coastal plain areas enjoy relatively good rainfall and plenty of lovely sunshine. On a yearly average, Darwin gets 8.5 hours of sunshine per day; Perth, 7.9; Brisbane, 7.5; Canberra, 7.2; Adelaide, 6.9; Sydney, 6.7; Hobart, 5.8; and Melbourne, 5.7.

The northerly parts of Western Australia, Queensland and

35

the Northern Territory are tropical and experience regular cyclones during summer. In Western Australia and Tasmania the annual rains fall mainly in winter: so they have cold wet winters and warm dry summers. For the other cities on the coast, it is the opposite way around: winter tends to be fine and dry and cool, while summer is hot and, the further north you travel, increasingly overcast and stormy. The desert areas are prohibitively hot in summer but glorious in winter, with crystalline days and frosty nights. The weather is more than usually important for the tourist, when planning an itinerary, in that the main sights are outdoors.

These simple guidelines might be useful: avoid Tasmania, Victoria and Western Australia in winter; avoid the Northern Territory, the desert and the tropical part of the east coast in summer; go anywhere at all in the glorious spring months of September–October or the autumn months of April–May.

Several other general geographic features might also be noted here. First, this is the oldest, flattest exposed surface of the earth. The general height above sea-level is a mere 300 metres; the highest mountain, Mount Kosciusko, reaches only 2228 metres. Second, and connected, is the dearth of major waterways. Certainly, the Murray/Darling river system ranks among the world's long rivers, but it is never a great river in the sense that the Nile is great, or the Danube or the Amazon. It never attains majestic width or momentum. The body of water remains modest, not unlike the Thames, for example. There are hundreds of small rivers, especially around the coastal regions, but they are short and erratic. Though prone to sudden violent flooding, they are, for most of the time, characteristically rather low on water. There is even a river in southern New South Wales (in a farming district) called Dry River.

Space is the property commonest of all in the Australian outback. And this has a profound effect on the people. With

5 Experiment Farm Cottage, built by a surgeon on land at Parramatta bought from a convict farmer, now looks out over the encroaching suburbs instead of wheat fields. It stood on the first land grant made in New South Wales in 1792. The cottage has been restored by the National Trust of Australia

6 The front entrance of the joss house, built by Chinese gold-miners in 1860, in Bendigo, Victoria

7 A country house in the grand style: Mount Pleasant, near Bathurst, New South Wales

8 In cane fields near Childers stands this typical Queensland house

an average of only two people per square kilometre, privacy is probably easier to obtain here than anywhere else in the world outside Antarctica. We tend to spread ourselves. Apart from the old suburbs in the main cities, where immigrant settlers built the style of house they had been used to at home, our suburbs spread immensely wide, giving most people room to have a fully detached house in its own garden and room for the car.

When the British moved in, the country which they took to be largely uninhabited was, in fact, completely occupied. Aboriginal tribes had adapted to living in every environment it offered, from coastal forests to grasslands, from deserts to the snow country. Each tribe moved throughout the year round its prescribed territory, harvesting the sparse crop of edible indigenous vegetation and killing as much as was needed of the wildlife in order to survive. They lived well off a land in which the white man, despite his knowledge of science, would starve.

The key to understanding the fate of these original inhabitants lies in what I have just called their 'prescribed territory', the sacred limits of their tribal districts. Aboriginal religions were – and in some areas, still are – animistic and anthropomorphic. The land is their kin. A mountain might be a hero of previous times who has lain down to rest after striking fire from the centre of the earth; a valley might be the dent left by his sleeping wife. The trees have personality. The animals and birds are cousins of man, who takes them as totem signs implying a deep family bond. It has been my great privilege, over the years, to have been shown something about the land by Aboriginal friends. One story will suffice to make my point.

I was walking through the bush with an old man. We didn't talk much, but we were enjoying the walk and the companionship. Soon we would stop for a drink. The sun was high overhead and hot. Suddenly his hand reached out to arrest me, mid-step. His movement was so swift but so fluid that it wouldn't have startled a bird. I froze. We stood still while he signalled with his eyes and showed me where to look. Something was there among the tufts of grass. I thought it must be a snake. But I could see no snake. I stood in the hot sun, not daring to speak, gazing in the direction my companion indicated. Then a cool breeze blew in from the west and he relaxed. He smiled at me triumphantly. 'Did you see him there?' he asked. 'Who?' 'That was my uncle. Uncle Jack.' Then he realised I had no idea what he was talking about, that I had not seen what he had seen, let alone Uncle Jack. 'Oh,' he mumbled apologetically, 'you would have called it the shadow of those leaves in the grass.' We walked on. 'The wind blew him away,' he added.

Whatever else was in question, there was no doubt the spirit of his uncle had been with us. He told me later that the whole bush was alive with his relatives, but that Uncle Jack was his favourite uncle and the one who had taught him most. Later he showed me a sacred cleft in some rocks. Also a distant mountain, the top of which, at that time of the afternoon, was clearly a giant face.

The fact that such monuments are natural phenomena is precisely what makes them miraculous to the Aborigine: they have manifestly never been carved or otherwise tampered with by those who hold them sacred, never reshaped by human hand. This is what vouches for their sacredness and proves they were put there by divine power.

The difference between Aborigines and the colonists who arrived from the British Isles was never more profound than in their mutual inability to perceive what was sacred to one another. These holy places were not man-made, and this was why the European mind could not (and still cannot) accept them as other than a category labelled Nature. There is, even

38

today, a profound scepticism in the white community about the declaration of Aboriginal sacred sites in our National Parks and elsewhere. Meanwhile, many Aborigines, for their part, dismissed Christianity as mere dabbling in magic because its shrines and symbols were so obviously the fabrication of human artisans.

Another difference arose from the newcomers looking upon the land as a resource to be cultivated and quarried. By contrast, the black people never took that critical step from use to abuse; they survived by attuning their society to the land as they found it. Though they undoubtedly had plenty of inter-tribal fights where they shared a boundary with neighbours, they knew every square metre of their home ground, knew exactly where water was and which plants flourished in which parts, they knew it historically and mythologically, it was their mother and its special forces were known only to them. The surviving records of tribal conflict – mainly caused by one tribe being forced off its land by the colonists and driven into alien country – show how unwilling the Aborigines were to leave the safety of their own sacred places and meanings. They had no concept of war as such. They had never united as an army and such a possibility probably did not occur to them. Even more astonishingly, they set no value on material possessions, though they lived on a continent rich in gold and jewels. Nowhere has a single article been found to suggest they ever made a treasure of these things, nor even ornaments from them. Their treasures were the huge languages of sacred words all committed to memory and transmitted orally and their art, which comprised a blending of painting, dance and song. Incidentally, if people doubt that there is anything remarkable in this, I suggest they pause and think again: one of these languages, which German Lutherans began transcribing last century, is estimated to having perhaps as vast a vocabulary as is contained in a large two-volume English dictionary. All memorised!

Basically, throughout the 40,000 years we know they have been here, they did without cities, villages, or permanent shelters. A couple of isolated stone structures have been found by archaeologists in recent times, dating from 1500 years before the Great Pyramid of Cheops – the exact site has been kept a closely guarded secret while the find is uncovered and protected – but in so huge a country and across such an unimaginable prospect of history, this isolated instance simply makes the absence of anything else the more starkly amazing.

Where did the Aborigines come from in the first instance? is not a question they themselves would ask. In their view they have always been here, though they fall into at least three distinct racial types. Of all the thousands of religious stories handed down in their great oral tradition, every single creation story is firmly set in this land. Can there be any other country on earth where the same people have lived continuously, isolated from invasions, for two thousand generations?

One may illustrate the difficulty of imagining such a period by returning to my example of the Egyptian pyramids. If we accept them as ancient (built some 4500 years ago), these people look to a past folding back this unit of time not just once but nine times.

The Aboriginal population today is estimated at just under 200,000, which is about 1.5 per cent of the total population.

Aborigines are not a tourist exhibit. We have no circuit of reservations where they put on corroborees or paint their bodies for outsiders to stare at. Here and there around the country one can find small shops set up by Aborigines in which they sell artefacts. But these are not especially distinguished – unless in the quality of delicate basketwork –

when compared to the great arts they practise for themselves, the song-dance ceremonials and the bark or sand paintings.

Tourist literature frequently features Aboriginal motifs and I think it is best to be clear from the outset that this is shameless exploitation. My guess is that the majority of Australians have never met an Aborigine and those living in the big cities have seldom even seen one in the flesh. A powerful undercurrent of guilt about the way these original inhabitants have been disinherited may equally well express itself as interest in their present welfare, or aggression, or outright racism.

The state art galleries in each main city own examples of Aboriginal painting and carving. Like their counterparts in Africa, South America and New Guinea, these works show a wonderful vitality, a sureness of purpose and refinement of line and colour. The two bark paintings by Yirrawala in the first room of the Australian National Gallery at Canberra are clearly comparable in quality to the Monet waterlilies and the Rubens portrait which hang on the adjacent walls. Any exhibition of Aboriginal art advertised for commercial or public galleries is worth a visit. Even those painters such as Albert Namatjira who have adopted European materials and the European tradition still produce works of remarkable individuality and liveliness. Of course, as with any community, this reputation in art has led many untalented Aborigines to put brush to canvas or paint-stick to bark and produce inferior works, which are readily available for purchase by the public. But doubtless the buyers get pleasure from them all the same.

In some remote areas tribal people still live by their traditional skills and retain their immemorial beliefs relatively unaffected by all that has happened here since the 1788 invasion. Fathers still take their sons, and mothers their daughters, teaching them how to hunt, teaching them the sacred lands – the areas for different totem groups and places of unique power which the young may not go near though they are told that special food and animals live there. Over and over the same ground, the children are guided. They must learn every detail in all seasons until, at about fifteen, they are ready to be initiated and taught the meaning of these sacred places, being entrusted with words that only the initiated know.

They are also taught an oral history telling, among other things, of tribal wars. 'In a big war,' as the story is told by a wise old man I know from the Northern Territory, 'three or four people might be killed.' A battle of this sort was witnessed by Andrew Petrie near the centre of what is now Brisbane. In 1904, his son Tom recorded the story in his reminiscences, telling how spears were thrown and the art of dodging them expertly demonstrated – until one man was killed, which decided the outcome by showing whose spirit ancestors were most powerful in that place, so the conflict was called off. Amazing to think that this could be laughed at as primitive by persons whose own history glorified a catalogue of the bloodiest conflicts not even resolved by hundreds of thousands of deaths. The deciding of the tribal fight wasn't the end of it, however; after the combatants had taken a break of weeks or even months, there began a cycle of reprisal killings against those who had struck the fatal blows in the pitched battle, and then against those who killed *them*. Again, though the process could go on for an indefinite length of time, the fatalities were on a small scale.

This oral history extends right up to the present, from tales of missionaries (both good and bad), to the arrival, typically, of bulldozers crashing through the bush, violent and unstoppable as tanks, smashing down sacred trees while blasts of gelignite blow the tops off sacred mountains and huge mechanical scoops are driven in to gather the rubble of a whole people's past for crushing as minerals so that the desecration can be measured on profit graphs at the Sydney stock exchange or some head office in London or Tokyo. Such oral history has to account for the people of the land being simply kicked aside, protesting and pleading but not being heard, venting their anger violently, perhaps, and still not being heard.

How does a history recognise the impotence of its own tellers? How does it begin to conjecture what will happen once the traditional ceremonies can no longer be performed in a place where they have any significance? How can it surmise the fate of children whose parents are left with nowhere to take them when the time comes for initiation? What happens to a race who, after 40,000 years of walking where they liked, are now shut out by fences, jailed and even shot at if they try scaling the fences and returning to the land that was always theirs, that in their own mind has never ceased to be theirs and for which no one among the usurpers signed a treaty or made the least gesture towards recognition of prior ownership?

Here and there, tribal councils are set up by the white administrators and the people of the land are invited to elect their representatives – a concept as foreign to them as, say, Japanese imperial court protocol might be to those of us who expect them to embrace this system despite having had no education into how it might work. Such councils are then invited to present submissions on issues (generally concerning the further disposal of their lands), or on the administration of cash grants. Meanwhile, in the general community, resentful citizens vent guilty consciences by protesting against what they call the squandering of tax-payers' money on Aboriginal affairs.

It is a difficult and tragic situation – difficult for us and tragic for the Aborigines. This is no South Africa, legislating

43

for two nations within the same boundaries. The black people here are a tiny minority. Without power of arms or the threat of sheer numbers, they have become dependent in their struggle for justice upon how far an enlightened pressure-group of whites can make inroads into the megalithic greed of other whites. And the greediest among us would appear to be those whose life's productivity consists in manipulating stocks and shares.

In 1987 an Aboriginal spokesman made world news by appealing to the Libyan leader, Colonel Ghadafi, to take up the Aboriginal cause and exert pressure in international forums to try forcing the Australian government to stand up against powerful sectional interests within the country and address the problem of how to resolve the situation with justice. Ghadafi's very name is, of course, a red rag to the capitalist bull. But the tactic may well prove to have been justified. The issues are unresolved, and they go right back to 1788. The whole point is that no war was ever formally declared or acknowledged on the British side. Australia was occupied as if it were uninhabited, although right up till the late 1850s there were more black than white people here. There has never been a treaty. The undeclared war was fought – no doubt about that – but without a peace agreement to settle hostilities.

To this day, the Aboriginal people have never surrendered, which raises ticklish issues. And when a group of notable citizens (including Dr H. C. Coombs, as retired Governor of the Reserve Bank of Australia, and the distinguished poet Judith Wright) formed a committee and worked strenuously to galvanise public opinion to call for a treaty, they were met with blank indifference. The committee, despite its high associations and invaluable work at laying out the issues, eventually disbanded four years after its formation. The work, however, has not been in vain. Judith Wright wrote a splendid book on the history of that four-year campaign, which will doubtless someday provide a blueprint for successful action.

Meanwhile – and it is an exciting development – Aborigines are taking their future into their own hands and declaring that, if necessary, they are prepared to appeal to world opinion. As things stand, such racism as there is in the country tends to remain under cover of a general tolerance, surfacing only in times of stress. Also, the problem is not often visible in the cities, because by far the majority of Aborigines live in country areas. But the question is one of basics and it won't go away simply because it is uncomfortable.

It would be a great education for all Australians, whose notion of Aborigines is of a few despairing drunks hanging around hotels in the seediest parts of our towns, to see them among their own people, relaxed and laughing in the acceptance of an extended family, or out in the bush, well fed and at home in country which, to our eyes, may look featureless and waterless.

Aboriginal technology was extremely limited, but one concept, the boomerang, has added a very effective image to the international vocabulary. The other main development was the woomera, a spearthrowing device which works by simply lengthening the hunter's arm (a concept so beautifully simple and effective one wonders why it was never thought of by the Romans or Chinese or Incas). At one end of the woomera is a notched nub on which the spear haft rests, the other end is held in the hand. The velocity of a spear thus thrown was very considerable and its range fell not much short of the flintlock muskets that were set against it in the early colonial days.

The problem of arms and the incompatibility of cultures was obvious from the first. That brilliant navigator and

45

humane son of the Enlightenment, Captain James Cook, had this to say of the natives of New South Wales:

> They may appear to some to be the most wretched people upon the earth; but in reality they are far more happier than we Europeans; being wholy unacquainted not only with the superfluous but the necessary Conveniences so much sought after in Europe, they are happy in not knowing the use of them. They live in a Tranquillity which is not disturbed by the Inequality of Condition: The Earth and sea of their own accord furnishes them with all things necessary for life; they covet not Magnificent Houses. Household-stuff, etc; they live in a warm and fine Climate and enjoy a very wholsome Air: so that they have very little need of Clothing and this they seem to be fully sensible of for many to whome we gave Cloth etc to, left it carlessly upon the Sea beach and in the woods as a thing they had no manner of use for. In short they seem'd to set no value upon anything we gave them nor would they ever part with any thing of their own for any one article we could offer them. This, in my opinion, argues that they think themselves provided with all the necessarys of Life.

We enter a wholly different world when we hear the other side of such incidents, a world of powerful unknown forces, the freakish, circumscribed world of belief in magic. According to recent accounts of Aboriginal oral history, the presentation of a shirt was a mystery which the local people were afraid even to approach.

> ... and they got a big long stick and they picked it up with the stick and they couldn't make out what that was. They thought this man was changing his skin. They said this man left his skin there. They said this man has been peel

himself like a snake and they got the stick and they picked it up with the stick and they looked and looked at this shirt and trousers ... But when he took his shirt and he was white they thought he change his colour when he took his shirt off. They pick up that shirt with a stick because they was too frightened to pick it up with a hand because in our custom might be something very dangerous, witchcraft.

In Aboriginal culture, white is the colour in which the dead come back. In rituals, faces daubed with white clay signify the dead. So this pale aspect itself was a further cause of fear. But once they began to realise the strangers might simply be people as human as themselves and people, moreover, intending to stay, they fought back. An incident during March 1789 was instructive. A group of convicts who believed one of their fellows had been speared by natives set out to exact revenge. Armed with nothing but staves and lumps of wood, they so deeply believed in their superiority, they had no doubt of victory. Fifteen of them went and eight returned. One lay dead and six badly wounded. The gentry in whose service these convicts laboured then took it upon themselves, accompanied by some redcoats armed with flintlocks, to teach the tribesmen a lesson. Had they come into open conflict, they might well have found their weapons gave them no advantage, being clumsier and far less accurate than spear and woomera. But they had an unseen ally on their side – the irrational. Whereas the soldiers surely knew the inadequacies of these temperamental firearms, the Aborigines did not. A stick was held up to the shoulder, gave a flash like lightning and a bang and (at least sometimes) something fell dead: plainly, it was magic of a terrifyingly immediate kind. Like guerrillas the world over, when confronted by a superior force, they simply melted into the landscape and were nowhere to be seen.

For this, they were dubbed cowardly and treacherous – such is the logic of propaganda.

When I was learning Chinese I asked my teacher what the writing on his calendar said. He gazed a moment at the bold characters painted down the side of the picture. 'Do you want to know what it says, or what it means?' he asked. 'Let's have what it says first.' 'It says "The Great Lake has no farther shore," which means, "One is not advised to plan too far ahead in life." ' I often think of that when I consider the dilemma of the Aborigines. Not only is English a foreign language to some of them still, but, by definition, a foreign mode of expression too. The language they must cope with, as an occupied people having no choice in the matter, is as remote from their own meanings as Chinese is from ours. When educators express concern at the levels of Aboriginal illiteracy (which are certainly higher than they ought to be) they would do well to bear this in mind.

We must keep reminding ourselves that, as Professor Henry Reynolds puts it: 'The courage of European explorers pushing out into the interior was matched by that of the Aborigines who ... travelled in towards the white men's settlements to observe and evaluate the interlopers. Epic journeys of discovery were not the preserve of white men.'

An overwhelming proportion of the Aboriginal stories – so far as we can gather from what they are willing to share with us – concerns origins. They are sacred creation myths. I read several thousand of them while editing a comprehensive anthology of Australian poetry, and almost every one reaffirmed anthropomorphic connections: showing the land forms as petrified totem ancestors, as part-animal / part-human, in the act of laying down the rule of law by which tribal society survived successfully, often in very difficult conditions, for several thousand generations. No mean achievement. This alone should give the outsider pause before dismissing the stories as childish or quaint.

Earlier this century a British anthropologist coined the term the 'Dreamtime' for this age of transmuted elements, when birds became people who became rocks or trees. He later regretted the term. And so might we all. The Dreaming has become commonly used – even by many Aborigines themselves – giving a wholly false impression that their oral tradition is some kind of hallucinatory wishful thinking, when in fact it is the most solid, tangible form of history imaginable. You can go and climb a mountain which was once your ancestor who defeated the lizard people; you can bathe in a river which they gouged as they died; you can pick fruit from bushes marking an escape route of people in direct communication with the great spirit, the maker of thunder and lightning and rain.

No place is richer for these myths made manifest than Uluru (Ayer's Rock), the entire mountain being one whole, compound, singular story in stone. A detailed account of it was published by C. P. Mountford over thirty years ago and reissued in 1965. It takes a full book. To give a very brief outline, the rock embodies events of a great battle between two snake peoples, the Kuniya and the Liru. The Kuniya lived in that place and, as boulders, they still do. The caves are their camps and waterholes. The Liru, led by a great warrior, Kulikudgeri, came first upon a group of women. A powerful woman called Pulari, who had just given birth to a baby which she was desperate to protect, spat out the spirit of disease which killed many of the attackers while she escaped with the child. Then a young Kuniya warrior, a kinsman of hers, challenged the great Kulikudgeri to single combat. The marks of their struggle may be traced in huge gouges and weatherworn indentations on the rock. Eventually

Kulikudgeri struck the fatal blow and the young Kuniya man crawled away across the dunes to die. His tragic death was immortalised as landscape in three waterholes created by the pools of his blood; while Kulikudgeri stands by, as a huge square boulder.

The complexity of the story, the moral entanglements, the epic search for a just solution which could never be found and, above all, the vivid characters, make this a myth worthy of comparison with the *Odyssey*. But it has yet to find its Homer whose genius is equal to setting it down in print in its own Pitjantjatjara language.

The unique quality of Aboriginal stories is best conveyed by their living ceremonies, the great corroborees combining dance, song and body painting, the scent of the land in swirling dust and, after dark, the action fitfully floodlit by the light of a central campfire. But this is a privilege available only to those who commit themselves to the Aboriginal cause or those rare white people who have come to share their way of life. However, an important element of this authentic feel may be gleaned from bark paintings and these are to be found in all state art galleries as well as in those remote areas where they are still being painted.

More will be said on this subject in the chapters on Western Australia and the Northern Territory.

I do not wish to give the impression that one moves from white-inhabited areas to Aboriginal-inhabited areas by simply travelling far enough inland; merely that the further inland and the further north you go, the more likely it is that you will encounter Aborigines among the people you see. There are only very few pockets of the continent where white people have not yet found the means of extracting profit in one form or another: mining and tourism having now opened huge areas previously left alone because of their unsuitability for agricultural purposes.

Mind you, these agricultural purposes are pursued in some fairly unlikely-looking territory all the same – especially beef cattle raising. Even the fringes of Sturt's Stony Desert can be used for cattle if the grazing area is vast enough to support the herd. There are parts of Clifton Hills Station (in such a totally flat area, the name alone is astonishing) on the Birdsville Track which test one's credulity. Even so, the fact is undeniable. And the farmers who live and work in these remote regions are interesting to talk with if you ever get the chance.

For those visitors who decide to venture outback and are not deterred by the great flat spaces, the harsh heat or the world's friendliest flies, the area around Broken Hill, overlapping the borders of New South Wales, Queensland and South Australia, has much of interest to offer. Not only Lake Mungo, as mentioned, but outlying sheep and cattle properties. The best way to get an idea of life in these parts for the non-Aboriginal is to take the mail plane. For about $70 you can enjoy a unique day. The four-seater aircraft, flown by a local chemist each Saturday, calls at some twenty stations. The price of the flight includes morning tea at one homestead and lunch at another. The pilot is a companionable Dutchman who simply loves what he is doing. You fly in a great arc out across the country, hopping up and down to deliver mail into mailboxes set up at each station airstrip. Most times the owner or some member of his family is there to say hello and remark on the hopeless fineness of the weather (if ever they get enough rain out there it is a flood and everything drowns), to smile at you, to give the pilot letters for mailing when he gets back to town, perhaps to ask him to take a parcel a couple of stops further on to a neighbour who needs the contents rather urgently. And up you go again, the Dutchman pointing away ahead to the right to a just-visible clump of unconvincing-looking trees grouped, apparently, around a house. 'That's the next stop,' he says. And you watch the bare flat country creep beneath you, an occasional steer not interested enough to raise its head, an isolated dam or bore water tank with a star of hoof-beaten tracks leading to it from all directions, but no sign of life, and wonder how in the world the farmers run enough beasts to earn sufficient to stay alive. Then you look ahead and the next station homestead appears no closer, so you can get a feel for how far away it must be – and there lies the answer. They run maybe one head of cattle per ten acres of land. It seems a doomed enterprise, though. This country had no indigenous animals with hooves. The grasses and thin topsoil are fragile. Sheep, cows, horses and pigs have kicked and trampled it to dust. In places they have literally created desert. So the herds range over colossal areas to find enough feed to sustain them and, in doing so, reduce the grass-bearing capacity of the soil for the future.

Still, when you arrive at that next property and find it enclosed in a startlingly green garden of shady trees bordered by bright phlox and salvias, the gateway embowered with roses, and sprinklers turning lazily on the lawns, you realise some families not only manage to make a living, but have become rich out there. The garden is sustained on artesian bore water, the shafts sometimes needing to be sunk 1500 metres deep before tapping the water table.

The time I took this flight, morning tea was served at a depressed looking place, a low-set, simple fibro house appearing much the worse for wear, with rusted fly-screens right round the verandahs and a muddle of decayed machinery in the yard, sump-oil in rank puddles among the skeletons of old army surplus trucks. The land, looked at from ground-level, appeared scrawny and featureless. On the western horizon a sullen line of squashed hills showed up, their bare stony tops appearing to only just break through the soil. Not

9 Artists at work on bark paintings, Maningrida, Northern Territory

10 Prayers at the mosque in Shepparton, Victoria. Most of the worshippers are farmers or orchardists from the local Albanian community

11 Flat horizon: part of Clifton Hills cattle station at the edge of Sturt's Stony Desert, South Australia

12 The delicate tapestry of a backwater off the Murray River, Victoria

an animal in sight apart from the usual bevy of noisy house dogs.

Our host kicked his heels as he made clumsily to usher us through a small wire gateway and over the hard dry soil to the back door. Inside his wife welcomed us, though too shy to look me in the face. Her kitchen was large and simple, with lino on the floor, a cheap clock ticking on a shelf above the sink, and a flight of those china ducks I never thought I would ever really see in anyone's home fleeing east along one wall. She opened the oven and brought out several batches of scones.

On this flight there were just the two of us. Sometimes the pilot is by himself, sometimes he has three passengers. Plainly, I thought, she expected a party. She poured tea and set homemade jam and luscious fresh cream for us. We were running late so we were hungry. Having tucked in to the scones, the lady then produced a monumental fruit cake and began carving bold slices from that. The pilot gave me a warning glance, which I could not interpret. I accepted the cake. These outback people began to relax with me and soon we were talking quite freely. Now came the most astonishing thing. The dogs barked and a knock came at the front door. A simple thing like a knock at the door in those parts seemed in the furthest degree bizarre. The farmer thought about it for a moment and then got up. We heard his voice and one other. The two men came into the kitchen together. The newcomer introduced himself all round as the new regional officer for the plague locust control board. He was very young and unaccustomed to his big boots and broad-brimmed hat. He hadn't quite got the hang of at what angle to wear the hat so that it wouldn't interfere with his spectacles. The farming couple received this information without a blink of surprise or scepticism which I thought was very sociable of them, especially when he began to show off with a little bit of scientific advice he hadn't been asked for. 'And what do you think of your boss?' the host inquired. 'A good man,' the youth asserted without hesitation. 'He knows his stuff.' 'I think he's a dill,' the host said quietly and flatly and then went on to explain how he had spotted huge grasshopper breeding grounds over on the Stony Rises and reported them – and how no action was forthcoming from the department. Afraid they would take wing any day, he pleaded for immediate help because (as he explained to us) you have to get them while they are still hoppers before they're fledged. Once they can fly it's too late. Then they began to move, advancing in a line several kilometres long. This was the perfect time for wiping them out. But still the young man's boss prevaricated and claimed that it was against all probability for locusts to breed in the Stony Rises in the first place. Duly, the insects took wing and a new plague was declared. 'He's a dill, that's for sure,' the farmer insisted.

This began some wonderful reminiscences between him, his wife and the pilot, with me chipping in occasionally to help keep the party going. I was thoroughly enjoying myself. It culminated in the pilot's account of flying through a grasshopper swarm a few years previously. 'They were so thick, they blinded me,' he told us, 'a dense cloud of wings. I couldn't see where I was going. I flew lower and lower to try to get beneath them. No good, still blinded. Then suddenly I saw, right under my wheels, the roof of the homestead I was making for. I pulled her back up and hopped over with no more than a couple of metres' clearance, I'd reckon. That was the last time I'd ever try that. It hasn't happened again, but if I ever do hit a locust swarm, I'm going up, up as high as I can.'

We got going again, with a few more calls to make before lunch, which was at a big wealthy place and served at a huge table with the owner's extended family plus a couple of

54

jackaroos. (Jackaroos are horsemen who work on a property, usually with a view to treating it as a sort of apprenticeship toward becoming station managers later on – very often they are nephews, or second cousins, or sons from neighbouring properties.) The meal turned out to be vast: heaps of roast beef, gravy, greens, mountains of roast potatoes, the works. All in the middle of a hot autumn day. The moment I sighted the loaded plates I knew why I had been given those warning signals over that cake I had eaten no more than an hour previously. There was no help for it, courtesy required that I do justice to the hospitality. I told the Dutchman I thought I could hear his plane groan as we took off for the afternoon's deliveries and the flight back to Broken Hill. All in all, it was a memorable day, which I would recommend to anyone.

This story reminds me of a general point I'd make to visitors who wish to get the most out of their trip. It is essential to mix with people, not to set yourself apart from them, to talk with them without quizzing them about what they do. By far the best way to elicit information is to be ready with stories of your own to tell. Anecdotes about close shaves always go well. Nothing makes friends quicker than reminiscences about one's own failures. The instant the company laughs at what you say against yourself, their reserve will vanish and they will open up. Australians are basically generous and gregarious, but with a distinct prickliness if they feel the slightest condescension is there.

3 Hauntings from Gold Rush Days

There can be no doubt that nature is the star attraction in Australia. Whatever else may be offered as a bonus, again and again one turns to nature for the most memorable experiences. I mentioned earlier that a fine way of entering Victoria is via Echuca, the old Murray River port. This was where the great cattle routes from Queensland and the Northern Territory converged for crossing the river. Last century, a cable ferry operated here, large enough to carry a couple of drays, complete with teams of twenty bullocks. Wool shorn on properties throughout the great inland plains was also brought here in bales and loaded high on barges to be transported hundreds of kilometres down to the river mouth and thence to world markets: timber barges floated by themselves (each barge guided in the slow-flowing river by the simple device of trailing a length of enormously heavy chain) to be claimed by sawmillers downstream when they saw them drift into view.

Travelling from the flatlands around Hay and Deniliquin in New South Wales, one approaches the Murray with a sense of relief. No matter how gratified the eye has been by the long prospect, in that country of distant horizons, the river is life-giving and gentle.

Echuca was lucky enough to have fallen into the doldrums long enough for people to begin caring about what remained of the old town. It was not knocked down in the scramble for 'progress'. Many of the river port buildings still stand and the restoration process has still not managed to correct all signs of wear and tear, or suffocate under layers of fresh

56

paint and chintzy décor what was often endearingly ugly and
battered. A good part of the original four-level timber wharf
still stands, with port offices grouped around it. There are
also some fine houses in the town and a pleasant, casual
atmosphere.

Several paddle-steamers still ply the river for a hundred
kilometres up or downstream; these days, entirely for the
tourist trade. My wife and I took a sample two-day cruise on
the PS *Emmylou*, a delightful little vessel carrying sixteen
passengers. Though housed in a diminutive cabin, we were
well looked after, with plentiful food and friendly service.
The trip was very expensive, but the experience well worth
it ... for the nature-lover. If you don't like looking at
innumerable trees, herons, egrets, flocks of black cockatoos
and king parrots, as well as the chance of sighting a rare
platypus hurrying down the muddy bank to slip under the
surface, don't bother.

During the whole trip a few houses are passed, but very
few and very small, one or two boats might come by and one
or two people might wave from the bank. The rest is nature.
And nature seeming, at first sight, to repeat herself. It takes
a while for the eye to become accustomed to differentiating
fine shades of diversity. But by that stage, the pleasure is all
the greater. One can lounge in a deckchair, reading, and
occasionally look up to find the river banks consistent yet
new, very much the way a fine novel turns its basic theme to
the light of intelligence, revealing a hundred permutations of
the one style. I found the result a charming colloquy, the
river and the fiction (Henry James, in this case) unfolding
side by side, while the pressures of everyday life wafted
further astern, mingled with steam and wood smoke from
the boat's furnace.

When evening comes, with the slow quiet river swimming
past to the cackle of kookaburras and the homing screech of

57

the last few cockatoos, a special magic begins. As the daylight fades, the steamer's spotlights are turned on. How much more marvellously deep and clear the water appears after dark. No longer brown and shallow, it is black and deep enough for the tallest trees to stand reflected there to their full height. The double image, floodlit, reveals that unnatural aspect of its beauty which we recognise immediately as essential to our idea of glamour. The pleasure of this night journey is hard to overstate. For that reason it is best to make the trip when the days are not too long – ideally in April, May or September (the service does not operate during July when the weir system for the huge Murrumbidgee Irrigation Scheme is opened); on a summer's day the boat will have reached its overnight tying-up point well before the sun sets.

Dinner on the second night is a bush barbecue with a campfire and vegetables cooked in a pit of hot coals. Very enjoyable for those who like the outdoor life – and, once again, better when summer is over and the mosquitoes are not too much of a plague.

One word of advice, though; if you are a vegetarian or cannot eat pork, I'd suggest notifying the operators well in advance because the meals are prepared as family meals, no choice being offered.

Back on the road again and heading south-east from Echuca towards the goldfields area around Beechworth, there are two stops not to be missed: Byramine Homestead near Cobram and the All Saints vineyard at Rutherglen.

Byramine, the oldest homestead in this part of Victoria, was founded in 1842 by the explorer Hamilton Hume for his widowed sister-in-law who, to judge by her photograph, was a tough old bird. She set out from Gunning in New South Wales on a 520-kilometre trek to her new home. Only one white person had been there before – Hume himself. She took her nine children, some tradesmen to build and manage the station, servants, and an Aboriginal guide known as Wellington. As soon as they arrived, a saw pit and brick kiln were set up and the house built to an English design especially developed for use in India. Not only was it to be cool in summer and warm in winter, but to convert easily to a fortress in case of attack from resentful natives.

The house is still there in its original condition. Such restoration as has been done is sympathetic and does not interfere with the pioneering defensiveness of the place, nor the simple sturdy structure. Designed round a group of three octagons and shaded by a broad verandah surrounding the whole house, the dimly lit rooms are of interesting shapes and pleasing proportions. But beyond this, the quality which captivated me was stepping straight into a very particular past, a past of danger and hope, as remote as one could well imagine from the comforts of civilisation. The homestead, overhung by two great elms planted in 1842 and a native kurrajong, speaks of the heroism of its owners as well as their ruthless invasion of the district, which they gradually cleared for pastures and reshaped for their own profit. The plain utility of the place, in an excellent state of repair, preserves the spirit of the pastoral age which suffered its severest blow a mere decade later with the discovery of gold and the arrival of tens of thousands of diggers from all parts of the world.

The distinguishing character of the All Saints vineyard is, similarly, connected to work. Unique among the wineries I have visited, one walks across the cobbled floor, right in among the casks. In this vast brick shed the cool air is faintly and deliciously soured. It is a working space and has not been tarted up or cluttered with plastic comforts. To taste the wines, one is invited to stand by a bare table and choose from the vintages available according to a blackboard propped against one of the casks. The wines are superb and winemaker George Smith is justly proud of them. The expertise of the staff and the atmosphere of the place make it a thoroughly enjoyable visit.

The area is among the most interesting in the state. Between Beechworth and Echuca the land has been rich in associations since pioneering days: farmers producing wool, bullock drivers transporting it by dray and boatmen taking over for the journey south by barge, involving the growth and decline of river ports along the Murray; miners digging gold from the ground and bushrangers stealing it. The associations are there.

News of gold being found in Australia reached London on 3 September 1851 – only three years after the first great discovery of gold in modern times at Sacramento Valley, California – and the gold rush began. Within ten years the colony's population had risen from 405,000 to 1,145,000 and in Victoria alone, not counting the New South Wales goldfields, the diggings were richer in yield than those of California during the 1850s.

One of the key towns was Beechworth. So ostentatious was the wealth that when Daniel Cameron campaigned for a seat in the newly formed legislature, he was said to have ridden through the streets of Beechworth at the head of a procession of richly apparelled miners on a horse shod with gold shoes.

The standard measurement of a town's importance in those days (and to some degree in these days) was the number of bars it boasted. When Beechworth's population reached 8000, there were sixty-one hotels, which rated pretty highly. The core of that flamboyant expansion still remains as an attractive town nestled at the foot of the hills. The most interesting relic is to be found in the cemetery. Among the graves of 2000 Chinese gold diggers stands a pair of 'burning towers' built in 1857. They were not, as many presumed, used for cremating bodies. The mourners burned paper prayers in them and meals for the dead. This indicates a large concentration of southern Chinese among the diggers who came, because in the north of China such offerings are usually burned at the graveside and not in towers.

As a footnote, I might mention that staggeringly little is known about the Chinese who came for the gold or actually migrated. They made important contributions to the founding of Australia as we know it today, but our history books tell us exclusively of European settlement, plus a tiny, apologetic summary of Aboriginal society prior to 1788. Records must be available somewhere in China, and many of the graves are marked. Indeed quite a few corpses were exhumed long after burial and taken home to China once their families could raise enough money to have this done. It is the wish of all Chinese to be buried in China. Behind the burning towers an altar was built later, in 1883. The inscriptions, when translated, read:

The public graveyard of those of all ranks, position and relationship of all the provinces of the Kingdom of China.

This stone was erected on the fourth day, being a lucky day, of the second month of the ninth year of the Emperor Kwang Hsu (c. 1884).

With the respect of those of the Prefecture of Canton and that south of the mountain range and the neighbourhoods thereof.

There was once a working temple in Beechworth too. One may easily recapture what it must have been like by visiting the joss house at Bendigo, 260 kilometres to the west, where this establishment is still operating after 130 years of continuous service to the traditional Chinese community of the area. The Joss, incidentally, was a regional Taoist deity. The step at the front door and the screens placed just inside were there to trip and thwart demons, who always travel in straight lines at the one level.

The Ovens River valley in north-eastern Victoria is a well-known tourist area. In April, the small town of Bright is transformed to a show place as the chestnuts, elms, scarlet oaks and poplars lining its streets glow and flame with autumn brilliance. Only in Canberra does one see a finer fall display than this. Just how exotic such a sight appears in Australia might be difficult to imagine for anyone who has not been here. Our native flora does, of course, change subtly with the year. But, except in spring, this is not a general and inescapable phenomenon as it is in most other temperate climates. The European or American visitor may well be puzzled at how little difference he can see in the same piece of bushland visited in April, July, October and January. Indigenous trees are not deciduous. Though they may shed their bark (and this in its own right may be a beautiful sight, as I have already mentioned when discussing the spotted gum forests of New South Wales), there is no flamboyant dying of gold, brown and red leaves. A gum forest puts on new growth in spring, crowning the trees with fresh copper and crimson leaves; gums also blossom on a showy scale; but we have no equivalent of winter bareness, the dazzling green pointillism of early spring, the thick shade of full summer, or the riotous ochres of autumn.

All the more vivid, then, are those places dotted round the country which were planted last century with British trees. Examples may be found scattered through Tasmania, South Australia, New South Wales (especially the New England Tableland and the Monaro) and Victoria. So it is that Bright, at the foot of the Victorian Alps, appears so colourful and so exotic. There is even a Festival of Falling Leaves held during

the last week of April and the first week of May. With
towering mountains for a backdrop, nestled in forest, the
town offers lovely walks to Clearspot and Huggins Lookouts,
while for those driving in the district, the Mount Hotham
road is especially favoured for the view of Mount Feathertop.
Tourists interested in quiet sporting activities could hardly
choose a better spot. In addition to the usual tennis, golf,
swimming, lawn bowls, fishing and boating, at Bright you
can go skiing in winter and flying in summer.

What distinguishes a city like Bendigo from the small
towns of Beechworth and Bright is that its gold lasted a
hundred years instead of a mere twenty or so. Certainly, for
the whole second half of the nineteenth century, Bendigo
flourished. The very layout speaks of its founders' pride and
expectations, with a 64-acre park in the middle and two
cathedrals. There are many showy Victorian buildings still
standing and the place is filled with reminders of past
opulence. But, to me, it has somehow lost its heart. When
these streets were alive with expectant crowds, the ferment
of rumours and news of fabulous nuggets, with business
people jockeying for advantage over one another, and all the
ebullience of expansion, no doubt it was an exciting place to
be. Now, however, the ostentation appears sadly unfunc-
tional, the community rather too placid, and the ornamental
architecture left without even a ghost of the high times it was
built to express.

A similar fate might have befallen Ballarat, but Ballarat is
substantially larger and the buildings a touch less quixotic.
The tone is less disillusioned if also, as a result, less interesting. On top of this, Ballarat got in first with a major effort
to capitalise on reconstructing the past, not just as bricks and
mortar, but as a living museum of work. At Sovereign Hill
an entire goldmining village has been reconstructed, its single
street a full-scale reproduction of Ballarat's Main Road as

this looked in the 1850s. Everything from mock goldmines to a bakery and a blacksmith's smithy operate more or less as they once did. In some instances, notably one apothecary's shop, entire walls of glass-fronted shelves and fittings are originals reassembled here, complete with printed information explaining how they were used. Citizens in costume stroll among milling tourists, an occasional horsedrawn cart rumbles by and a stagecoach arrives. The flag is hoisted or taken down, Clydesdales stamp their hooves and set shaggy fetlocks shuddering, school children rush from a gold-panning demonstration to the sweet shop, sightseers stream through gates and head for the quartz-crushing mill where a whim (a vertical winch) is driven by horses, puddling machines and cradles are racketed by cheery employees in rather motley stand-ins for the clothing of the period. Meanwhile, sated crowds of visitors push their way back out, linger in the souvenir shop or dash through a surprise rain shower to cars in the carpark.

Whereas I believe Sovereign Hill is entirely fascinating for school students, I wonder quite what it does for the adults who go there. Some, no doubt, are unsophisticated enough to accept everything at face value and come away feeling they have dipped into the genuine feel of times long lost. Others, I suspect, find it rather tiresomely nostalgic, rather shrilly chauvinist, and altogether suspect historically.

My own reaction was a mixture. There are certain things – tools, work techniques, items of furniture – which surprise and enliven the experience. An actual letter of the time, displayed in the photographer's window, speaks most movingly of the blessing of photography ... and one remembers that the camera was a new invention at the time and as much the rage as television is today:

Blessed be the inventor of photography. I set him above even the inventor of chloroform! It has given more positive pleasure to poor suffering humanity than anything that has 'cast up' in my time, or is likely to – this art by which even the poor can possess themselves of tolerable likenesses of their absent dear ones.

Mrs Jane Welsh
Carlyle 1859

Sovereign Hill is an odd mixture; some of it so carefully authentic, some mere play-acting. The lack of interest in getting details right concerning anything other than gold-mining, commerce or machinery – for example, speech, manners or music – simply raises one's scepticism to the point where it interferes with the pleasure in what is good. At least the central exhibit is an actual mineshaft from the 1880s, round which the idea was originally planned. The underground museum gives the best feel of discomfort in the whole enterprise. And discomfort is, I suppose, as good a starting-point as any if we wish to escape the superficiality of so much that is mere posturing.

This, at least, I can say to those with a taste for such historic reconstructions: Sovereign Hill is far better than its rivals, which one finds here and there round the country.

Ballarat's most famous incident, apart from the finding, in 1858, of the Welcome Nugget (weighing 2217 oz), was the only armed uprising ever to break out between whites and whites in this country. At the Eureka Stockade in 1854 miners fought as a protest against the licence fees. The uprising has become greatly magnified in the national consciousness to symbolise a whole philosophy of intransigence in the face of authority, a refusal to knuckle under, and a promise that, if pushed far enough, Australian workers will not shrink from defending their rights by violence.

The Eureka Stockade has long since outgrown the historical fact and become an event of far-reaching importance.

The riches from the Victorian goldfields flowed through Melbourne (as coal from the Latrobe Valley does today), which remained until very recent times the financial capital of Australia. And I had intended doing likewise on the trip I took to Victoria when I began preparing this book. But my plans were changed because I heard on the radio news that floodwaters were advancing on Dimboola to the north-west. It was some years since I had seen a flood. And I had never seen Dimboola. So that's the way I headed, determined not to miss the action.

The exact peak-time for the waters rushing down the Wimmera River had been forecast and were known by the townspeople. Embankments had been built hastily and motor pumps set up in low-lying areas to pump the water back over the levee into the river again. Trucks, loaded with emergency supplies of sandbags, were parked where the road dipped into the flood and the bridge could be seen just under the surface. People stood round, so calm as to seem almost indifferent. Some were carrying shopping bags, boys leaned on bicycles. A dog was sniffing the truck wheels. Even the air had a deathly stillness about it. The peak came, with an almost imperceptible rise in the level. But this was, nevertheless, the critical time. We watched the water creep up. One lady carrying a shopping bag shifted it to the other hand. The levee banks held. A few more sandbags were hoisted from the trucks and stacked on the weak points. Brown water pushed past, not at all spectacular in speed or even volume, so it seemed, and half an hour later began to subside very gradually – enough for a wet line a couple of centimetres thick to appear drawn along mud banks just above the water level. People began to disperse; some quietly, some with a joke, the boys showing a touch of disappointment.

I drove on, reminded about how resilient people are. At Stawell I had a different sort of reminder. One of the sights here is the 'Sisters' – great granite boulders, which will do as well as anything to jog our memory that the conflict between the preservers and the destroyers is not new. In 1867 some local residents saved the 'Sisters', which were marked for demolition in some urgent and forgotten cause. From this to the 1983 No Dams campaign in Tasmania and the fight to save the tropical rainforests of north Queensland and (such is the rapacity of industry) to save even the Barrier Reef itself from oil drilling, there has been no respite.

The mention of floods reminds me that I must also deal with that other most feared disaster, fire. The terror of a bushfire cannot be imagined unless you have been through one. Living in a remote and heavily forested area, as we do, the danger of fire is always lurking at the back of one's mind. The experience is frightening. First, to wake in the night to a faint smell of wood-smoke; and in the morning to see a smudge on the horizon and sniff a hint of aromatic eucalyptus oil (the same oil-particles that shimmer in the air and make the Blue Mountains as blue as they appear). Such fires travel so fast, the air itself seems combustible. The most feared bushfire is a forest crown fire, which rushes like a cyclone through the treetops. The smudge of smoke grows to a thick rolling cloud, rising and spreading, deepening and growing darker. Then an angry flush appears on the underside of the billows, a plum-coloured stain reflected from the unseen flames below. By nightfall the next night the whole horizon is a ragged black tree-line silhouetted against a bright orange glare. People of the towns and outlying farms pack their families and valuables in every available vehicle and drive clear of the danger zone; the men and many of the women then returning in groups to help fight the fire. Imagine a small country town at dusk lying in a valley, roadways completely empty, streetlamps twinkling, shopfronts illuminated and not a sign of human life anywhere. A single cat ventures along the tarmac and lifts its nose to test the acrid air. Beyond the surrounding darkness of hills a wall of flame advances. Nothing can stop it now. This is a sight which, once seen, may never be forgotten.

I cannot stress too strongly that, when travelling in country areas, one should never drop a cigarette butt or match, never light fires unless meticulous precautions are taken and the fire completely extinguished with water afterwards (burying often allows smouldering wood to stay alight, which may later be fanned into flame) and always observe the Fire Danger Indicators displayed by the roadside.

A fire I helped fight recently, near my own home at Bermagui in New South Wales, was started by a family having a picnic. At eleven o'clock that morning they boiled a kettle for a cup of tea. Six hours later, utterly exhausted, black from head to foot, eyebrows seared off, hands and faces scratched and scorched, trembling and in tears, they stood back with the score of local residents who had arrived to fight the fire and the area volunteer bush fire brigade to look at the smouldering wilderness they had created from a view they had earlier photographed as: 'So beautiful it made us want to stay here for ever.'

On 16 February 1983 (now known as Ash Wednesday) appalling fires swept through the Otway Ranges west of Melbourne and down to the coast at Lorne. More than 15,000 people fought the blaze – forty-five of them died; 1719 homes were destroyed; and 330,000 hectares of land looked as if it had suffered a nuclear blast. It has never been discovered who began the fire. But the bereaved families and the 8000 left homeless would like to know.

13 Tourists at the ruined convict prison, established in the 1830s, at Port Arthur, Tasmania

14 The main street of Richmond, Tasmania

15 One of the few inhabited buildings in the gold-rush ghost town of Ravenswood, Queensland. The steps to nowhere are all that remain of a once grand hotel

16 The old gold-mining town of Beechworth, Victoria

The special quality of resilience among rural communities has a great deal to do with the experience of such disasters. If there is an impatience with the trivia so many of us fritter our lives on – fussiness about our appearance, niceties of etiquette, an obsessive avoidance of the least discomfort – there is also a wonderful warmth and a sense of capability in the face of any emergency. Bush people pride themselves on their no-nonsense attitudes. Often enough, in those harsh surroundings, they have had little choice.

If asked what difference is to be found between one state and another – apart from differences of climate and landscape – I think the clearest answer is that they perpetuate (and even institutionalise) historic rivalries left over from the colonial era.

When the railways were being built, last century, the New South Wales government chose the British standard gauge of 4 ft $8\frac{1}{2}$ in. Victorians could not then have the same. How else were they to be sure all their trade would flow through Melbourne port and not be pirated by unscrupulous rogues known to constitute a voting majority in the neighbouring colony? They went one grander and opted for 5 ft 3 in. Queensland and Western Australia chose 3 ft 6 in., following the policy that they should build incompatible systems with anyone sharing a boundary with them. South Australia, uniquely, moved to solve this problem – the solution was to install all three.

Whatever rivalry might be felt between the other state capitals, the fiercest and most dogged rivalry remains that between the two biggest cities, Sydney and Melbourne. With a population of three million (only half a million less than Sydney) Melbourne prides itself on having all manner of superiorities – from restaurants to Australian Rules Football, to better public transport, a higher standard of political awareness and a far superior market for Rolls-Royces.

The first pioneer families moved into the region to escape what they saw as the dictatorship of the redcoat military governments both in New South Wales and Van Diemen's Land (later called Tasmania). Among them were men of property and tradespeople looking for room to expand. When Melbourne was established as the port for this area in 1837, a special relationship soon grew up between the town and the hinterland, a relationship which still exists. The inland cities of Bendigo and Ballarat have the character of flamboyant extensions of Melbourne. No other state capital enjoys quite this closeness to its provinces, nor quite the solid backing provided for so many decades during the great days of the goldfields. Yet Melbournians tend to look on their city with a mixture of affection and despair, rather as gypsies might view an aged relative who has settled down in a sober stone house to a routine slightly shameful in its respectability. Vehemently as they may claim superiority over Sydney, I suspect, being an outsider to both cities, that they nurture a secret longing to kick over the traces and live a life more like that of their raffish rival.

People in Melbourne have a preoccupied air. It is not just the weather – famous throughout the country for an inclemency almost as forbidding as the climate in the British Isles – it is as if each is, somehow, a person of consequence and in the act of conducting some unhurried business to the general benefit of the metropolis. This tolerant, modest, comfortable city does indeed have much to recommend it. The restaurants *are* the best and most varied Australia offers and the Art Gallery is far and away the finest. There is, perhaps, justification for the feeling one gets that the crowds in the street share a kind of pride. They intermingle like members of a club. Just as the focal point of Sydney is its harbour; Melbourne's focal point is its people. The 'club' is

70

united, I believe, by two things above all others – Aussie Rules (football), and a legacy from that mid-nineteenth century optimism when the city was founded, a faith in the common good, combined with the certainty that heaps of wealth could be dug from the ground by anyone with the will to go out there and give it a go.

The Victorian Football League grand final is one of the great events of the calendar, equalled only by another sporting event, the Melbourne Cup. To those not familiar with Australian Rules Football the name itself seems inappropriate. This fast, aerial game, more exciting to watch than any other code, including soccer, appears to owe its speed to the total absence of rules. It is a version of rugby and played with the same oval ball, but the spectacular leaps to score a 'mark' – with one player literally leaping up from the backs of his rivals to snatch the ball high in the air, with sensationally long torpedo kicks, no off-side rule, comparatively rare lineouts and no scrums. Flaunting a tradition of narcissistic male glamour, wearing sleeveless jerseys for reasons of freedom of movement and to show off their muscles, the teams race from end to end of the field to the concerted sighs and roars of 120,000 spectators.

Unlike other sports, VFL football (Aussie Rules, as it is generally called) does not look outward to national and international competitions. It is turned in upon Melbourne. It is a Melbourne phenomenon. And although in the past couple of years one team each has been fielded by Brisbane, Sydney and Perth, the league is still in Victoria and looks to Melbourne only.

Similarly, the Melbourne Cup is the one truly national horse racing event. Wherever you are – in the far west of Western Australia, in Queensland or in Tasmania, at 2.40 p.m. on the first Tuesday of November, you'll find the whole country comes to a virtual standstill. In 1987, even

71

during the world financial crash, the Melbourne Stock Exchange still closed for the usual holiday. Elsewhere, too, office workers desert their desks to listen to the radio in the tea room, shop and factory employees, managers included, gather round television sets and millions of dollars change hands through the bookmakers, the TAB (totalisator) and amateur sweepstakes. At Flemington race course the Royal Ascot tradition of dressing up has been taken to garish extremes. Men as well as women deck themselves in outrageous fashions, blatantly vying for notice; and each year, inevitably, a few of the most ostentatiously dressed are rewarded by being photographed for magazines and newspapers.

I do not want to give the impression that Melbourne is a brash city of show-offs, however, for most of the year it is quite the opposite – being rather staid, like a less industrial and sunnier Manchester. Indeed, Melbournians pride themselves on the discreet comfort of their life-style, rising to luxury for those who can afford it, a luxury which is symbolised by the exclusive Melbourne Club, also the Hotel Windsor, which advertises itself as 'Australia's Only Grand Hotel'.

Right in the heart of the city, the Windsor is our nearest approach to truly sumptuous accommodation. The exterior is a rather grim grey Victorian pile; but inside, guests find a warm atmosphere, the standard service runs to such niceties as your bed being turned down nightly and port and cheese placed beside it for a nightcap, afternoon tea being served in a lounge where you sit in leather armchairs among potted palms, dinner arranged on the plate as a picture of a butterfly alighting on a flower, a silver service breakfast, some quite respectable oil paintings around the walls, and the columns and ceiling roses in the public rooms trimmed with 24-carat goldleaf. Even the carpet itself is classified in its own right by the National Trust. It is not, I should also say in passing, wildly expensive; and rates very well as value for money if what you enjoy is being pampered by uniformed staff who park your car for you and bring it back to the front entrance when you are ready to leave, open the doors for you and wish you good evening sir/madam. A recommended way of sampling some of these pleasures at the Windsor for those who cannot afford to stay is to call in after the theatre for coffee.

Australia has a modest but solid theatrical tradition. Rossini's *The Barber of Seville* was produced in 1843, twenty-seven years after its first performance at Rome. By the 1880s, the late operas of Verdi were being seen in Sydney and Melbourne within four or five years of the world premieres. And Ibsen's play *Hedda Gabler* (written in 1890) was given its first English-language performance by the touring Janet Achurch company in Brisbane in 1892 – before it was known in either London or New York. The standard of theatre is very erratic, nonetheless. Seasons of the classics, such as Shakespeare, tend to be quirky and costumed without good reason in anything from modern dress to nineteenth-century top hats and spats, to frayed sacking. Perhaps the most solid drama company is the Melbourne Theatre Company. But personally I find their productions ponderously artificial especially when, as they often do, they try turn-of-the-century plays which require nothing less than perfect naturalness and an effortlessly light touch, such as those by Wilde and Shaw.

Australian plays are another matter. Visitors may sit in the darkened theatre, utterly mystified by what is happening all around them. A play – often of crushing banality – is in progress and the audience is letting out wild yells of appreciative laughter or sitting in that special resonant silence reserved for sacred occasions. I cannot answer this one. There are fine plays being written, such as those of Louis Nowra, but for the most part, mediocrity triumphs; and the public queues up for the novelty of seeing home-grown commonplaces in the glamour of artificial lights. The actors are often superb and far better than the material deserves.

I ought also to admit that I have similar opinions of the much-vaunted Australian film industry. There have been a handful of good serious films, one or two delightful comedies (such as Nadia Tass's *Malcolm*) and the occasional brilliant outburst of Mad Max violence, yet by and large it's pretty thin stuff – geared to appeal to a shallow level of social perception, based frequently on nostalgia – and might well pass unnoticed but for the tremendous amount of tub-thumping that goes on each time a new one hits the circuit.

My star rating I reserve for a good country rodeo, another of those Australian surprises not to be missed.

As far as Victoria goes, the special achievement is in dance. Melbourne is the home of the Australian Ballet and the three leading ballet schools, as well as a fine post-modern dance company called Danceworks. Apart from Graeme Murphy's splendid Sydney Dance Company, this is where you'll see the best dance in the country outside Aboriginal traditional dancing – which is one of the great experiences. The Australian Ballet presents lavishly costumed classical works, very much in the familiar mainstream. Their standards are high. Danceworks explores the dynamics of movement and produces exciting explorations of contemporary themes with an intelligence which sets their programmes well above the narcissism of much modern dance.

Having brought you to Melbourne, as it were, by the back door, approaching from the north, it remains to be said that this is a port; indeed, Canberra is our only major city which is not a port. The bay presents a massive, shallow, rather featureless expanse of sheltered water, around the shores of which lie everything from port facilities to sedate waterside suburbs such as Brighton. By contrast to the low-lying peninsulas enclosing Port Phillip Bay, most of the Victorian coastline is rugged, often inhospitable, and always beautiful.

The elaborate system of coastal swamps and tidal lakes extending right round the south-eastern corner of the continent are breeding grounds for the famous black swans. These elegant birds, true swans, have black plumage marked with handsome brown fringes and a bar of white on each wing which is revealed only when they fly. Their beaks are bright red. Flights of swans are quite common around this coastline. Some of the main stories of the Aboriginal tribes, whose remnants still occupy pockets of their hereditary land at Wallaga Lake in New South Wales and Lake Tyers in Victoria, relate to the swan. The Kulin people of Wilson's Promontory (the southernmost point of the mainland) tell of their primal ancestors Lo-An and his wife Lo-An Tuka who discovered the area and found it rich in birdlife, especially flocks of swans on the water. They fed so well on swan meat they settled by the shores of Corner Inlet and may still be seen at night just above the promontory looking out to sea as the stars we call Sirius and Canopus.

To my mind, the showpiece of the Victorian coastline is the Great Ocean Road. I'm not, on the whole, a lover of roads for their own sake, but this one is special. For 300 kilometres it winds along steep cliffs above the ocean, being actually cut into the cliff for much of the way, commanding spectacular views of wild forested bluffs and crashing waves. There are lots of places to stop and eat or rest overnight once you leave Torquay. Anglesea is pleasant. And Lorne is particularly lovely. (How the names of these Victorian towns tell their own story. Tasmania is the only other state where the names are so nostalgic, so infrequently touched by Aboriginal words or by other European associations, so doggedly Anglo-

Scottish.) Even when the road loops inland at Apollo Bay, the scenery has plenty of appeal because the way winds among treeferns through foothills of the Otway Ranges and into a temperate rainforest area. At Princetown, where it swings back to the coast, the most memorable part of the journey begins: once more along the cliff, this time following the edge of the Port Campbell National Park. A photographer's delight, the coast is gouged to dramatic shapes. Twelve great sea-girt towers standing out in the swell (predictably called the Twelve Apostles) make a truly magnificent sight, especially when the weather is moody and drizzly . . . which it often is.

Just beyond Warrnambool you find Port Fairy. Despite its being on the Princes Highway, Port Fairy still bears many reminders of the early whaling industry and is full of pretty, rather Devon-style stone cottages. Birdlife abounds, with pelicans and gulls and dotterels. No parrots, because they tend to shy away from the sea and the cold, and no brolgas either (the brolga is a crane-like bird famous for its courtship which takes the form of a ritual dance of extraordinary elegance): you have to go inland for birds like these. And it is well worth while to include at least a brief inland excursion in any travel plans.

At the back of the Great Ocean Road lie the rich grazing lands of the Western District, with sprawling station homesteads where, till recently, families with aristocratic British connections kept up their traditions of speaking French at dinner and occasionally having musicians to play in the ballroom gallery. The district is rich in lakes clustered round the largest of them, Lake Corangamite.

The late John Manifold, poet, folklorist, communist, broadcaster, Cambridge graduate and erudite black-sheep of his family, described the country on one of these properties as: 'plains, small declivities, all your rises and falls are kept within moderate bounds, and the horizon is a dado of nicely rounded hills, practically bare rock all of them – Mount Elephant is particularly beautiful from a distance, and one always remembers it as tawny-coloured, dust getting worse and worse as summer grew in, saltpan lakes; few trees and most of those planted.' (It was here that the fossilised remains of a giant marsupial, a wombat as large as a cow, were found.) 'So there was this classical landscape, everything perfect, and brolgas dancing. And, walking into our saltpan lake, the footprints of a prehistoric diprotodon. As summer drew on, with the diminishing level of the water, there were more steps after more steps. And then, dramatically, there was only a pool left in the middle and the end of the footprints.'

To the north-west the Grampians rise, mountains which are every bit as wild and impressive as their Scottish counterpart. The whole area is now a State Forest. Famous for wildflowers and birdlife, these rugged, wooded mountains are easily reached by road. The best place to begin exploring is from Hall's Gap where there are good motels and basic shops and services. Within easy reach are splendid walks and climbs and some breathtaking views from precipitous crags of rock that fall away beneath the viewing platform a thousand feet down to the valley. The tourist literature advertises plenty of wildlife to be seen, including kangaroos, echidnas and platypuses. All I can say is that I saw none of these; only a few delightful wallabies. Also I did hear possums in the trees at the back of the motel at night. Possums, like wombats and bandicoots, are very rarely seen by day. In all my years of bushwalking I have never once spotted a koala in the wild (in the Queensland chapter I shall suggest where to see them and even get to hold one) and, though I have come across platypuses in the wild, they are a fairly rare sight and generally to be found only in very secluded backwaters seldom disturbed by people. So I do not think it is a fair sales-pitch at all. These unique animals, egg-laying mammals, were extremely common when the pioneers first moved into the bush, but for 150 years they were ruthlessly hunted for their fur or as exhibits to be exported to foreign zoos and museums. We have only ourselves to blame that there are so few left. But I must make it quite clear that they do not lounge around waiting to charm the sightseer or pose for close-up photography.

As an aside, I might mention an occasion on which I actually saw two platypuses together. I had an overseas visitor with me. While delighted by what I was able to show him, he admonished me for my incorrect usage of the word. Not being a colonial himself, he had a fixed idea of the lamentable gap between his (superior) cultural inheritance and mine. The plural, he instructed me kindly, should be 'platypi' not 'platypuses'. Need I say, I was too embarrassed on his behalf to point out that the '-pus' root comes from Greek for 'foot', not Latin; that 'platypi' is not only pompous, but wrong. The plural of '-pus' or '-pous' is '-podes'. If one wishes to sound ridiculously academic, 'platypodes' is a better shot. But how you then get out of the problem of explaining that the broad feet ('platy-' from 'platus': 'broad') belong to more than one animal, I leave to you. Apart from 'platypuses', the other convenient plural is simply to leave it at 'platypus'.

My recommendation for this area of Victoria would be to stay at Glenisla station homestead. Run by its owners, Eric and Evelyn Barber, guests are treated as family friends, and offered plenty of good food, four-wheel-drive trips around this fine merino sheep stud (some 5000 hectares) and up to the Grampians. The owners will show you everything from wild emus and kangaroos – here you really do see them – to a lake with the skeletons of thousands of drowned trees jutting from the water. Dead trees are a very Australian sight. In some regions whole hillsides and paddocks are full of them. Mainly they have been killed intentionally by a process called 'ring-barking': a complete ring of bark, perhaps a foot wide, being removed from round the trunk to cut off the tree's life-line from its root system. Characteristically, trees killed in this way, right through from last century to the Second World War or thereabouts, have been left standing. It is a weird, haunting and, in its own way, beautiful sight. The homestead itself presents a marked contrast, being weighed down with luxuriant growth of wistaria and surrounded by exotic trees, cypress, mulberry and fig. The building dates from 1873 when it was a coaching stop *en route* from Melbourne to Adelaide. The house is filled with fine furniture and the fireplaces are of imported Carrara marble. Take your walking shoes and weatherproofs and I'm sure you would find this one of the most memorable, enjoyable and relaxing experiences on an Australian holiday.

There is, incidentally, a Host Farms Association offering details of many such places throughout the country, and is highly recommended.

Small though Victoria is in relation to the rest of the continent, this state offers a great deal of variety and interest. But without doubt the weather has to be a consideration. The climate is cool and damp. I am tempted to say 'miserable', but that is from the perspective of an ex-Queenslander living in sunny New South Wales.

4 *Almost Another Country*

TASMANIA

My first visit to Tasmania was when I went with my family to stay with the poet Gwen Harwood and her husband. The children were quite young then and tremendously excited; doubtless this excitement rubbed off on my wife and me as well. We flew from Melbourne. I cannot say whether Hobart and the surrounding areas would be as magical for a visitor who does not have a poet as guide, but I think back on this as one of the most memorable of holidays. One's second experience of going somewhere is seldom as vivid as the first. But this much I can say, after several subsequent visits, Tasmania is a wonderful place for the tourist, and the nearest thing to the sort of touring one enjoys in Europe.

The key issue is that the growth in population has been relatively slow. The island is about half the size of England, yet it has only 500,000 people. There has not been the same pressure of expansion as we have felt on the mainland; not the same call to knock down the old towns and build new, nor to bulldoze super highways across the quiet countryside. The history of Tasmania (and often it is a tragic history) has left its mark everywhere: convict jails at Richmond, Port Arthur and many other places, old coaching inns, churches, farmhouses and bars.

These historic buildings share some interesting characteristics. Although none is earlier than 1803, the year the colony was founded, they are nearly all unmistakably Georgian. This raises a point very useful to the understanding of Australia. The colonists who first came here brought with them an eighteenth-century culture. The Industrial Revolution and the French Revolution had not yet changed the face of European life. Especially the gentlemen adventurers, who tended to set the colony's fashionable tone, insofar as such a thing existed here, were great sticklers for a tradition in which the rural gentry had not yet been displaced by a class of manufacturers, where their workmen still acknowledged some personal loyalty to them and were known by name.

The rhythms of the machine had not yet replaced the rhythms of nature – a man could still sit down and rest when he felt like it, his productivity was elastic and his pace largely self-imposed, rather than being driven to keep to the machine's relentless pace. The colonists also brought with them an open hostility against the increasing high-handedness of the government in Britain during the slump immediately after the Napoleonic War. This outspoken antagonism, reinforced vigorously by Irish arrivals, still has echoes in our attitude to authority today. And poverty had, for the first time in modern history, become a burning moral issue with the pauperisation of British rural workers suffering under infamous Corns Laws.

But perhaps more profound in its influence than all this was the fact that to the eighteenth-century mind, land constituted the basis of power. Even in parliament, it was not people who were represented, but property. With this in mind, it is easier to imagine how boundless the possibilities in Australia seemed, how space itself came to promise social as well as physical freedom. One need only read the poetry of the first decades of the nineteenth century – Shelley, for example – to find how freedom had become a preoccupation of the new age. So, at the very time when England's population was rising alarmingly fast (it doubled in the seventy years between 1750 and 1820) and land was entirely taken up and monopolised by the wealthy, Australia opened her wide hinterland to the excited ambitions of explorers and the pioneer farmers who followed them. As country districts flourished, so did commerce in the towns. Revenue was created and people demanded comforts which they found they could buy without undergoing the trauma and upheaval of the factory and foundry economy that had taken over the homeland.

The touchstones of refinement were still Alexander Pope for poetry, Nash for architecture, Adam for interiors, Reynolds for portraiture, and a foreigner, Haydn, for music. The first English play to be performed on Australian soil was Farquhar's comedy *The Recruiting Officer*, written almost a century earlier in 1706. 1787, the year Governor Phillip and the First Fleet set out for Australia, was the year Haydn's publisher, Bland, invited him to England where his music was already all the rage. Haydn declined, on that occasion. But the following year he wrote a symphony later to be performed at Oxford, when he *did* pay a visit, and called 'The Oxford'. It has even been argued that the Australian accent is an eighteenth-century English accent (possibly a conflation of Cockney and Cornish speech), just as the American accent might, roughly speaking, be the English of the seventeenth century. Whatever the case, colonies are notoriously conservative in their tastes, manners and speech. In more recent times, the British in India have been famous for being more British than the British at home.

This quality of pre-Regency austerity is to be seen everywhere in Tasmania.

Where the mansions and public edifices are concerned, we cannot pretend the quality of design or craftsmanship equals that of comparable buildings in, say, Virginia, but lovely little buildings abound and Hobart's Salamanca Place right on the waterfront is a fine example of a street of the period. Since the early 1960s there has been a tremendous upsurge of public interest in preserving old buildings. They do tend to be rather too tarted up (as with the Rocks in Sydney), but the impulse is preferable to the wholesale destruction that has gone on elsewhere.

By far the biggest drawcard for tourists in Tasmania is Port Arthur on the south coast. Here stand extensive ruins of a huge prison, built to house 12,000 convicts.

We had a car at our disposal when visiting Port Arthur and this was a great advantage. We arrived early in the morning, as it is only 100 kilometres from Hobart, passing through attractive countryside on the Forestier and Tasman Peninsulas, with pastures, woodland, rocky coves and occasional ocean views. We were able to reach our destination before even a single tourist coach had arrived. The only people already there were two families who had camped overnight at Port Arthur itself. The great prison stood silent in the clean air, reflected by the water of the inlet. For a moment I believed it had been cleansed of blood. But then, quite suddenly, in one of those moving moments when we relive history, I felt the intensity of human suffering still hanging over the place, felt it envelop me, almost physically.

The appalling cruelty of the convict system is hard to credit. Flogging was a daily routine. The lash was administered to men spreadeagled on large timber frames called the triangles by fellow convicts, who were compelled to perform this task. To take one example: at Macquarie Harbour jail in 1822 (the year when Wordsworth published his *Ecclesiastical Sketches*, at a time when the first steamship had already crossed the Atlantic, when Faraday had invented the electric generator and Britain could regard itself as the most modern and humane of societies), in this distant corner of the empire, at this one jail, 169 of the 182 prisoners received 2000 lashes or more. That small band of felons, often transported for trifling offences in the first place, suffered a total of nearly 350,000 strokes of the whip during the twelve months.

Hardly less shocking were the working conditions. Convicts had been sent, after all, as unpaid (or enslaved) labour to build the ports and set up colonies as trading posts. It cost the Westminster government a hefty £17 per head to transport them. Once there, they worked six days a week for as long as the light lasted. Limepits may still be seen where they cut and burnt lime for mortar, and quarries where they toiled removing and dressing the stone for their own barracks and detention cells as well as for harbours, churches and administrative buildings.

The chief industries in the early days were whaling and sealing. In the years when Van Diemen's Land (as Tasmania was called originally) was being set up, the profits from whaling alone have been estimated at £200,000, an enormous sum in those days. The Derwent River, on which Hobart stands, was a breeding ground for whales – long since wiped out or driven away. And Bass Strait, separating the island from the Australian mainland, swarmed with seals; so much so that sealers used to sail all the way from America for the rich pickings.

The peninsula is very nearly an island. It is connected, at the landward end, by an incredibly thin neck of sheer rock called Eagle Hawk Neck. In convict times guard-dogs ranged the area, secured on running-leads to a line stretched from one side of the narrowneck to the other. The line was also patrolled by guards. No prisoner ever escaped by land, though a few braved the wild ocean and the danger of sharks to swim to freedom. The panorama from Eagle Hawk Neck is breathtaking, looking out over a wild, rugged coastline where there is scarcely any sign of settlement.

When returning to Hobart, it is only a twenty-kilometre detour to visit Richmond. Here again, the visitor must watch

17 Grape pickers at Mt Prior vineyard, near Rutherglen, in north-east Victoria

18 The flamboyant Marble Bar, now in the Sydney Hilton International Hotel, having survived the move from the old Adams Hotel

19 Desert landscape near Alice Springs, Northern Territory: foothills dotted with mulga scrub give way to the Macdonnell Ranges beyond

20 Terrania Creek in the Daintree Rainforest, Queensland

out for convoys of tourist coaches (unless actually a passenger in one). Tasmanians are tremendously proud of Richmond – and with some justification.

We reached Richmond in the late afternoon, just as the petrol fumes of the last departing bus were being blown clear by a stiff southerly. Bliss. The slanting sunlight, already a dusky gold, bathed the town in a wonderful warmth. Despite the little prison, where you can still see irons let into the wall, still read names scratched by hopeless inmates, the chief impression is the town's charm. No matter how often locals tell you the ghost of an overseer, murdered by the convicts, haunts the old stone bridge, the grimness will not stick. The jail, built in 1825 (five years before Port Arthur), and the square with its jailer's residence and court house are so beautifully laid out, so small and well proportioned, they outlive their original use. One sees them, free from torture and brutality, simply as architecture.

On a subsequent trip to Richmond, I discovered that by far the best way to approach the town is along the old Grass Tree Hill road, via Glenorchy and Risdon Vale. This road, built in 1832 and connecting with a ferry across the Derwent River, provided, for many years, the sole access to the area. Twisting and turning through the valleys, it is a route with a great deal of charm.

In this area, the so-called Tasmanian tiger was reported for the first time. The animal, referred to in a Hobart newspaper in 1823 as a 'striped hyena', had been found devouring a lamb which it had killed. Despite the strangeness of the wildlife encountered by pioneer farmers, one thing had become clear – apart from snakes, sharks and a few spiders – none of these native creatures need be feared. Docile koala bears and timid wallabies were accepted as fair game for the shooter, though harmless in themselves. So, one may imagine how sensational such news was: an animal as big as a medium-sized dog, viciously savaging and killing a lamb.

Of course, it ought to have been clear that there were not many of these predators, since none had been sighted before, though settlers had lived in the district for twenty years already and were within a year of seeing the Richmond town site declared. But this is not the way with people's fears. The alarm was out. And from then on the hunt became official. Classified as a dangerous beast, the objective was to wipe out the so-called 'tiger'. A couple of them were caught and put in zoos where they soon died. The rest were shot as marauders. So it came about that this extraordinary marsupial, like a small wolf but with a pouch for its young, a unique animal, is now extinct. Though many expeditions of naturalists have hunted the wild highlands for evidence of survivors, they have had no luck. The last known specimen died in captivity in the 1930s.

Apart from a wealth of simple, sturdy, sandstone houses with carefully fitted flagstones, tasteful mouldings, and twelve-paned sash windows, there are a couple of really handsome residences on a more substantial scale: a magistrate's house from 1831 and Belmont homestead.

Saint Luke's Church, small and austere, is a joy to visit. The original cedar fittings and furnishings were, unfortunately, remodelled in the 1860s, but the materials were re-used and, although the high-backed box pews built for the gentry have gone as have the rough benches provided for convict worshippers, the present pews were fashioned from the same timber with the result that, apart from the addition in 1865 of some Victorian English stained-glass windows, St Luke's can be seen much as it was in Richmond's heyday.

I've left the bridge till last – for the usual reason. It is the finest building in the town and one of Australia's little treasures. Begun in 1823, and finished two years later, it has that organic feel which only age and use can give: strict lines now sagging slightly, and the stone courses acquiring a sinuous undulation. The basic structure of five stone arches is well proportioned and solid. The prow-shaped pylons (too thick and too high ever to be thought elegant) were needed for withstanding the powerful flow of water which, in a wet season, can come rushing down the valley through that normally quiet backwater of a river.

So much for the sights. Having seen them, most visitors return to the city as their base. But often the hospitality in these little places amply rewards the decision to stay there overnight. An attractive place to choose in Richmond is Prospect House. That is, if, like my wife and me, you enjoy restored farmhouses and old bars. Prospect House restaurant specialises in game dishes. On going there, I must say I rather relished the whole scene: dashing indoors from a cold drizzly evening to find a cheerful fire crackling in the grate, leaning on a marble fireplace while thawing out, settling down to thick hot soup, followed by potted duckling. 'There are', we said to ourselves, 'worse fates one might suffer than this.' A charming old building, accommodation is available, but for weekends you need to book well in advance because, being so close to Hobart, it is a favourite weekend holiday spot for locals.

In fact, Tasmania has a chain of such bed-and-breakfast places dotted around the island. Known as the Tasmanian Colonial Accommodation group, they make a selling point of tradition: the old buildings and family-style breakfasts. In Australia, unlike Britain, B & Bs are fairly rare, so it is all the more of a change to make the most of them in Tasmania.

Hobart itself is an attractive little city built round a beautiful deep-water harbour and dominated by Mount Wellington. The original wharf area is still used and, being right in the middle of the town, gives it a distinctly old-world feel. When the weather clears there is a pleasant walk to be had via Kelly Steps from Salamanca Place on the waterfront to Battery Point, the oldest residential district of Hobart. Apart from tarred roads and fresh paint, this area is much as it always was. An ideal climax to the day of sauntering around is to dine at Mure's Fish House, perhaps the finest seafood restaurant in Australia – and that's saying something, with the superb quality of oysters, prawns and crabs available everywhere, and the fantastic variety of fish.

A few illegal casinos operate in various parts of the country, but Hobart was the first Australian city to open a legal one. Other States followed. Now casinos operate in Adelaide, Darwin, Perth, Surfers' Paradise and so forth. But the one at Hobart's Wrest Point has the best setting, right on a lovely cove where hundreds of yachts are moored, masts gently swaying to the movement of water and the stays and lines jingling and slapping.

I must confess to a blind-spot, however. Personally, I find casinos and nightclubs the most tawdry and boring of entertainments, so I cannot hope to do justice to describing this one for readers who might be interested. I have been there. The place was moderately busy. Customers dressed in everything from evening gowns to sun frocks, and from lounge suits to jeans and sport shirts. They seemed to be having terrific fun. I tried my hand at roulette and baccarat. This was mildly enjoyable, as all gambling is, but I couldn't stand the assault of the decor, the music, the smoke, the company, or the atmosphere. I got a lot more of a kick, I must say, when I took part once in an illegal two-up school in the yard at the back of Watson's Bay Hotel in Sydney.

Two-up is an Australian game, simple-minded in itself, but rousing the onlookers and gamblers to a boisterous involvement. The game is controlled by a 'boxer' who supervises the spinning of two coins, traditionally pennies. The player called the 'spinner' tosses them in the air, using a little wooden spatula, the 'kip'. He must call heads. The other assembled players bet against him or against each other, throwing their stakes on the ground. The head side of each coin is usually polished to make identification easier. If they fall as one head and one tail, this is called a 'no throw' – only two of a kind count – so the spinner must try again. Two-up has an extraordinary vocabulary of terms, for such an elementary game: 'ringie', 'alley-clerk', 'alley-loafer', 'sleeper-catcher', 'head' and 'mug' for the players; and terms such as 'nob' for a double-headed penny and 'grey' for a double-tailed one. The moment the pennies soar in the air, the cry goes up 'Come in spinner!', which has become a national saying for anyone who falls for a swindle or makes a foolish decision. A dressed-up version of the game is offered by most casinos, including the one at Wrest Point.

The Tasmanian Museum in Hobart has the best exhibition of artefacts from the convict era and is well worth a visit. But beware of the information given about the supposedly extinct Tasmanian Aborigines. I have met a few! Disgraceful as the official story is (an account of 'benevolent' genocide, a succession of failed attempts to foil the social Darwinism of a 'superior' society wiping out a 'primitive' society), the present shame is that this version allows people to ignore the plight of the descendants of those tribes. On much safer ground is the exquisite display at the Allport Museum, housed in the State Library building. This is a tiny museum of eighteenth-century furniture and porcelain. The high quality of the pieces, and their display in the context of fully furnished rooms, makes a most interesting and tasteful collection.

Driving north from Hobart through the Midlands region, one sometimes has to blink to be certain this is not England, the very same late eighteenth-century England of the Chippendale and Sheraton furniture at the Allport Museum. With staggering energy, the early colonists set about the task of clearing the land of every trace of native growth. They transplanted the trees they loved and created a rural landscape as a faithful replica of the one they had left behind on the far side of the world. Freestone walls and slate-roofed stone cottages offer reminders of the Cotswolds. The farmhouses stand in little gardens of sweet-williams and stocks, hollyhocks and rambler roses. Along the roadside occasional hawthorn bushes have been trimmed by some volunteer amateur topiarist to fanciful shapes, as cockerels and urns. No greater contrast could be imagined than the untouched landscape of the Tasmanian central highlands and the wilderness of the west coast.

Another comfortable establishment listed by the Tasmanian Colonial Accommodation group is Hillview House in Launceston. Launceston tends to get overlooked in the scramble for superlatives. Yet it is a pleasant town on the banks of the Tamar River, the setting-out point for anyone wishing to visit Cape Barren Island (flying in a tiny plane over the astonishing mauve fields of flowering lavender), or to cross the island to visit the fascinating myrtle forest of the north-west corner, or, nearer to town, pleasant little villages like Evandale, near which stands Claremont, the only mansion comparable in style to those palatial Georgian piles in Mississippi. Behind the pillared portico, the rooms are few but handsomely proportioned, and the whole place exudes a stylish airiness.

Cradle Mountain may be approached either from Devonport or Burnie. The area is famous for its bushwalks, the most demanding of which is the Overland Track, 85 kilometres long. The area includes one of Australia's strangest forests: the native myrtle. Rich in that haunting quality of a children's book illustration, trunks and branches are covered with moss and lichen. Yet the forest is not dark. Its foliage, being delicate, lets in plenty of light, but the light shows up the strangeness of twisted trunks, and the forest floor as a mat of tangled roots which have killed off all sign of under-growth. The myrtle forest is extraordinarily quiet. Occasionally a single bird call will be heard, but seldom an answer. Even wind passes through the forest silently.

Cradle Mountain is a splendid rocky pile, jagged and imposing, in a National Park which extends for 50 kilometres south to embrace Lake St Clair. This is another superb spot. The lake, known to be over 200 metres deep, lies tranquil in a basin gouged by glaciers 20,000 years ago. Its southern shore is easily reached by car, being only six kilometres from the Strachan Highway, the main road running diagonally across the island south-east to north-west. The area around Strachan and Queenstown is one of the highlights offered by an Australian tour.

For a combination of natural grandeur and the tragedies of colonial history, this Tasmanian west coast is hard to beat. Queenstown clings to a mountainside which is utterly barren, all vegetation having been either cut down as fuel or poisoned by a century of sulphur fumes from the silver-lead smelters at Mount Lyell. Bare stony slopes, rising above the town, appear burnished, a curious blend of coppery pinks. Though there is a modern mining operation still working the tin underground, much of the old town remains.

An island in nearby Macquarie Harbour was once the most savage of all penal stations. This was where the worst of the convicts were imprisoned, where those 350,000 strokes of the lash were given in a year. The headlands at the mouth of the harbour were known as Hell's Gates. Very few convicts ever escaped and among those who did there were tales of cannibalism being used as means of surviving the wild seas and the equally wild land.

We now see this wilderness through different eyes.

Only once in the history of Australian federal politics has an ecological dispute been a real vote-catching issue. It happened in the 1983 election. The Australian Labor Party gained a lot of favour throughout the country by its stand against the state government over the issue of preserving this wilderness area of the Tasmanian west coast and stopping work on the scheme to dam the Franklin and Gordon Rivers. A *No Dams* campaign was mounted nationally and aroused a huge amount of support. In consequence, these beautiful rivers still rush down through thick forest and deep ravines despite the outcry of the 'developers'. The wilderness has become a notable tourist attraction and white-water canoeing and rafting are now offered as popular sports in the area.

The surrounding mountain ranges rise, almost impenetrably wild, to rugged peaks where there are still residual stands of the famous huon pine, among the longest-living trees on earth, much sought after for their timber. It was to fell these trees that the convicts were originally sent to Macquarie Harbour because, as always, the free labour was directed toward a desired product. The huon pine has become something of a rarity and is now protected.

Anyone attempting to explore the area will find the going extremely rough. In addition to which, the weather is habitually wet and cold. This is the most inhospitable climate in Australia and presents an extraordinary contrast not just with the palm-fringed shores of tropical Cape York, or the red sand of the central desert, but with the warm, gentle coastal plain on which most Australian cities have been built.

Travelling north from Queenstown, you come across a number of other mining centres, the most memorable being Zeehan. Five kilometres to the south is Mount Zeehan, which was sighted and so named in 1642 by the Dutch explorer Abel Tasman. (It was in 1856 that the name of Van Diemen's Land was changed to Tasmania.) The mountain was found to be rich in silver-lead. Mines flourished and the town grew until, by 1899, it had twenty-five hotels and a population of 10,000. Full of the usual swagger associated with boom towns, they also built a huge theatre. At the time it was the largest anywhere in Australia. The Gaiety still stands as a cavernous musty relic of forgotten good times. The front portion of the building, housing the box office and administrative offices, is of brick and has an exuberant façade mixing Dutch with Italian styles, while the auditorium behind is built of timber and galvanised iron. Dame Nellie Melba, no less, once came to sing there.

Each time I go to Tasmania I am surprised afresh at how different it is from the mainland states. It feels like another country. On the one hand, the reminders of Britain are so much more marked than anywhere else in Australia; while on the other, the wilderness is so much more bleak and harsh resulting from the cold weather. The same cultural shift occurs in reverse, upon returning home across Bass Strait.

5 The Best Laid Plans ...

ADELAIDE ~ SOUTH AUSTRALIA

Australia is not, as is sometimes claimed, a classless society. There is a clear division between the middle class and the working class. But what is true is that Australians show very little interest in class as such, only in the money and comfort that go with it. An upper-class accent tends to be thought of as a liability, a quirk to be mildly ashamed of – certainly not flaunted.

Within this general observation, one must make a marginal exception of South Australia.

From the day of its foundation, South Australia was set up as a gentlemen's colony. No convicts were ever shipped here. Adelaide was established in 1836 by Crown Land being sold at sufficiently high prices to put it beyond the reach of immigrant labourers, while allowing some of the profit to be used for financing the passage of more such labourers to serve the interests of the well-to-do. This was the nearest approach to a successful transplantation of British social strata. The scheme worked as planned, at least at first; and the principal business in South Australia became real-estate speculation – thereby giving the dealings of a century and a half ago a surprisingly modern flavour. Within eight years, the new colony was earning substantial returns from the rich copper mines at Kapunda and Burra – once again providing a pointer to the way the whole country's economy might develop.

Adelaide people still carry with them an air of being chosen leaders, of being more cultured and more comfortable than other Australians. Not surprisingly it was Adelaide which, in 1960, set up the nation's first world-class arts festival. Modelled closely on the Edinburgh International Festival and under the guidance of Professor John Bishop of the Conservatorium of Music, the festival flourished, to be given a huge boost by the building of a theatre complex which, when it was opened in 1972, was described by the *New York Times* as 'one of the world's great theaters'. Held biennially, on the even-numbered years, the programme has grown to include such star attractions as the Royal Shakespeare Company, the Israel Philharmonic Orchestra and the Bunraku Puppet Theatre of Japan.

Festival time, in March, is definitely the choice time to visit Adelaide. The city turns on a wonderful show, with programmes including opera, ballet, drama, and mime, children's activities, exhibitions, an international writers' festival, and a host of fringe attractions. The restaurants and accommodation in the city are good and the atmosphere is excitable. You can walk anywhere from anywhere (the city being exactly one mile square and flat), and the pleasure is topped off with reliably fine weather.

Even so, if I had to nominate Adelaide's special privilege I would choose neither its festival – admirable and enviable as that is – nor its gentlemanly past and tidy planning, but the arrival midway through last century of a whole community of German immigrants. These immigrants established vineyards along the Barossa Valley to the north of the city and McLaren Vale to the south. The glory, still, of South Australia is its wines. And a most enjoyable holiday can be had by hiring a car to drive yourself around the wine-growing districts, calling at vineyards, tasting their vintages, buying an occasional bottle, and staying at small country inns. (The one stricture to bear in mind is that Australia has severe penalties for driving under the influence of alcohol.) The beauty of the area for a holiday is that the places of interest are all so close together. My advice is to avoid the big company firms. Every Sunday, crowds take day trips from Adelaide and cram into the reception halls of the Orlando, Seppelt and Penfold Wineries and taste one or two standard whites and reds, take it or leave it, served in horrible little plastic cups. Because the samples are free, the assumption is that most visitors simply intend getting tipsy in good company at no expense to themselves. These big wineries do produce superb wines also, but you can't get a taste of those by just fronting up at the counter with the horde. By contrast, the smaller, family vintners do have bottles of their good wine open. They offer it to you in proper glasses and will discuss what you might choose for drinking with your favourite foods. The best value of the Barossa, I found at Saltram's. Not only is the reception hall a pleasant old stone barn of a place, but the wines are excellent and the staff extremely knowledgeable and welcoming. Though I had no intention of making a purchase, I ended up by buying two cases of their Pinnacle Selection Sauvignon Blanc (1982). I have regretted it ever since – I should have bought far more. For tasting reds, my choice would be Chateau Reynella in McLaren Vale.

South Australians, as a rule, take their wine seriously. Whenever you eat out in Adelaide, you may be reasonably sure the restaurant will carry a good selection. But, owing to the heavy tax on alcohol, they are not cheap by British or American standards.

The secret of enjoying Australian wines to the full is to remember that, though they are labelled according to the grape variety (and these are often familiar in France or Germany) the wine is not necessarily an attempt to replicate what may be produced at Bordeaux or Bingen. South Australian shiraz, pinot noir, or whatever, may well have its own character and needs to be appreciated for this. Visitors prone to perpetually comparing everything they find with what they

96

have 'back at home' are likely to cut themselves off from much that is enjoyable, simply for the satisfaction of seeming to know best.

The wine industry has an interesting history. Governor King decided, in 1800, to combat the colony's drunkenness and the use of spirits as a currency, by planning for the production of wholesome wines and beer. He arranged for two French prisoners-of-war (from the Napoleonic War) to be brought to New South Wales to advise on cultivating grapevines. A year and a half later, 12,000 vine cuttings from France were planted. The basic stock supplied subsequent vineyards in the Hunter Valley, in Victoria and South Australia. They flourished. So much so, that when the phylloxera plague struck France in 1863, devastating many areas, Australia was able to export cuttings back to their place of origin to help re-establish the stock.

Beer – amusingly enough, for a nation of beer drinkers – came a little later. The first brewery began production at Parramatta in 1804. Nowadays, when so much beer is produced by international combines, who often seem more interested in take-over bids for each other than actually brewing the stuff, it is reassuring for visitors and residents to discover small, local, independent companies dedicated to excellence. Just as Californians, who still have taste-buds, can enjoy Anchor Steam Beer brewed in San Francisco, so in Adelaide may be found the family-owned Cooper's Brewery, set up before the First World War, and justifiably proud of its Cooper's Sparkling Ale, still bottle-fermented – a method familiar to the growing number of home-brewers.

If you approach Adelaide by road from Victoria, you can drive along the Coorong, which is, perhaps, the most publicised of all our bird sanctuaries. But untouched wilderness it certainly is not. When I was there, I took this road, approaching from the east. I stayed the night in Kingston,

97

sharing a particularly grim motel room with about five hundred mosquitoes, who apparently found it as difficult to sleep there as I did. Setting out next morning far earlier than was my habit, I comforted myself that all would be for the best because this gave me a longer day exploring the dunes and lagoons and observing wildlife. It did give me a longer day, yes, but a day with plenty of disappointment, as well as pleasure.

The Coorong, another name for the Younghusband Peninsula, running parallel to the South Australian coast, stretches with threadlike thinness for 145 kilometres. Between the peninsula and the mainland lies a lagoon no wider than many a river and reputed to be infested with birds. I saw scarcely a single one. Well, autumn must be the wrong time of year. I don't doubt there are whole flocks to be seen in spring.

The one crossing from the Princes Highway (which defaces the shoreline the whole way and supplies the area with homely noise-pollution and carbon monoxide fumes) is at 42-mile Crossing, midway between Tilley Swamp and Salt Creek at the Kingston end. You need to keep your eyes open for the sign, it can easily be missed, and this is the only chance you get, because at the western end the Younghusband Peninsula pokes right out across the mouth of Lake Alexandrina, a huge shallow estuary rather like Port Phillip in Melbourne, and you end up with water all around you.

Having found the way across, the track leads through some interesting dunes quite densely vegetated and out on to a straight beach so colossal it vanishes to the horizon in both directions. At that stage, stand clear, because the shelly sand is used as a race track, the entire length of it being crushed and rutted by scores of tyre tracks. The local hoons burn up and down, trying out their four-wheel-drive vehicles at speeds illegal on the road. I walked for a while among the dunes and found it pleasantly easy to get away from the licit traffic of the highway and the illicit traffic of the beach, but I was aware that this illusion of wilderness was only an illusion and that by deviating 100 metres either way I could prove it.

Far more exciting, to my mind, and far less celebrated is the Flinders Chase National Park, a mere 100 kilometres further on, on the western extremity of Kangaroo Island. The island may be reached by vehicular ferry running twice weekly from both Adelaide and Port Lincoln. The terrain is wild and impressive and so is the coastline. I watched penguins and seals, neither of which seemed much bothered by being observed. Also I saw some of the rarer Australian sea-lions, though I cannot find any account of this in my notebooks, so I can't now remember whether it was at Hanson Bay or Seal Bay. Anyway, the whole area is worth a visit and, like so many places in this country, the more leisurely the visit the better it will pay off. There is also excellent fishing.

The weather in South Australia is probably more predictable than anywhere else in the settled parts of the continent. Summer is reliably hot and dry.

Not only can you sit in an open-air restaurant in Adelaide, feeling detached from, yet at one with, the passers-by – besides innocently eavesdropping on conversations taking place at neighbouring tables – you can do so with the assurance that you are less likely to be unexpectedly rained on than in any other Australian capital city. I had chosen a sunny spot at about eleven one Tuesday morning when a group of young men in business suits came strolling along the Rundle Street mall, exuding affluence and ease, junior executives, perhaps, or associates in a firm of solicitors. They sat right in front of me.

'... government department,' one of them said loudly.

'They specialise in absurd letters,' another agreed.

'Their day,' a third began to explain, casting his eyes modestly to one side as if to disown the appreciation certain to be accorded him, and by this simple gesture making clear that he was accustomed to being the star attraction at their leisurely amusements, 'their day in the public service is only one step down from vice-regal. You think I'm joking? No. Take my cousin. Typical bureaucrat. Gets to work in time for morning tea,' he broke off the narrative briefly, to order himself a Vienna coffee and two slices of pecan pie, 'then retires to the toilet with the *Sporting Globe* and emerges for lunch. During the afternoon he completes a report on the unemployed of the north-western suburbs which eventually passes over three desks and collects two appreciative comments before being filed under "U", never to be seen again.'

They all laughed hugely, leaning back in their wicker chairs, exposing their waistcoats to the winter sunshine and rooting about in their minds for another amusing subject with which to provoke the entertainer to further heights of extravagance while fresh coffee and cakes were brought by the waitress, a small Vietnamese woman who wheeled a chromium and glass trolley loaded with éclairs, Black Forest gateau, tarts and hot croissants. A suave, fashionable Vietnamese man strolled a pace behind her, overseeing the service and nodding to the customers. To and fro these two passed, visiting various tables, while the young solicitors vied for attention with moral horror stories of other slackers in the so-called working community.

Certainly statistics make nonsense of any claim to Australian classlessness. Five per cent of the population own ninety per cent of the nation's wealth. That is probably on a par with pretty well every other industrialised country. But the point is that this inequality carries little cultural weight and almost no taboos of status. The rich are not identifiable by their accent nor are they necessarily accorded any special

21 The inimitable grace of kangaroos in action

22 Cave painting by an unknown Aboriginal artist, found in Arnhem Land, 1948; exact copy made on masonite

23 Aboriginal rock paintings, Kakadu National Park, Northern Territory

24 Roman Catholic Church of St Peter & St Paul, built underground at the opal-mining centre of Coober Pedy, South Australia

social privileges. For example, in a bank or a factory the manager is probably addressed on first-name terms even by relatively junior members of staff. The fast-growing epidemic of tipping and unearned deference is eating away at this. There was a time, not so very long ago, when a male customer would be most surprised to hear himself called 'sir' except in the most exclusive hotels and jewellers' shops. 'Mate' was the universal form of politeness. And very warm it was. Even the great flood of European migrants in the 1950s did not dint this Australianism – the newcomers quickly adopted and enjoyed the casual mode. I think the change has come with the growth of tourism, with the increasing gap between poor and rich, and with the arrival of a host of Asians already imbued with fixed ideas of service learned in their own countries to satisfy the expectations of American visitors, military as well as civilian.

As a footnote, I merely record that on this particular Tuesday morning I was working on this book. When I left the restaurant at midday to pick up my hire car, the young men in pinstripe suits were still there exchanging witticisms about the sloth of the working class. The Public Service here, as in so many countries, is the butt of wildly exaggerated claims of inefficiency. Originally modelled on the British ideal, one could do far worse, desperate rearguard actions are needing to be fought to prevent governments from selling it off in bits: telephone service, health scheme, airports, and even the Australian Broadcasting Corporation are all under threat. These services, having done so well for us, it is no wonder the sharks want to get in on the act. I suppose even the post office is not sacrosanct either. Incidentally, as things stand, the hospitals are free and anyone, including visitors, may turn up at Casualty for treatment without cost.

Health standards, in general, are high and you need not worry that you are coming to a primitive country with poor

101

hygiene and a high risk of catching contagious diseases or suffering food poisoning from eating in restaurants. Even in the far outback, health care is remarkably good, including the famous Flying Doctor Service, an airborne rescue team in radio contact with settlements and properties throughout the inland, as well as helicopter rescue services in many coastal and mountainous regions, with the operators publicly funded and specially trained to cope with the terrain. Anyone who intends a long, slow exploration of the central desert, for example, can arrange to borrow a two-way radio, be given a personal call-signal and a check-in time, remaining in contact with civilisation and in reach of help should a crisis arise.

If you wish to see desert country and do not plan to include Alice Springs in your itinerary, Adelaide is the closest state capital for reaching this kind of area, as you realise the first time you step into the streets on a summer day when a north wind is blowing, bringing the smell of the desert, oven-hot temperatures, and a dryness sufficient to snatch the breath from under your nose. For a brief taste, a day trip is all you'll need. Or, for a longer look, travel to Port Augusta and use this as a base. The Flinders Ranges (not to be confused with the Flinders Chase National Park on Kangaroo Island) are very beautiful. The roads are quite good, but beware of taking dirt roads after rain – as in all semi-desert country it is easy to become hopelessly bogged.

This is an area perfect for walking, especially in spring when the wildflowers are out. A comfortable motel has been built beside the camping ground right in the heart of the national park at Wilpena Pound. This is definitely a recommended place to stay. The Pound itself is quite extraordinary. You approach a solid wall of mountains, cliffs rising 1000 metres from the plain, pass through a gorge of pink- and plum-coloured shale, into a great saucer-shaped depression. The vegetation and the surrounding mountains, not to mention the flocks of parrots, are a photographer's delight.

The traditional story of Wilpena Pound as told by Daisy Utemara of the Adnyamatana tribe concerns two giant serpents who journeyed there to destroy the people who had gathered for the first of all circumcision ceremonies. They hid, waiting till the ritual was over, then they surrounded the people, swirling round them so fast they created a whirlwind that swept them into their mouths. Three of the intended victims escaped: Wala the wild turkey, Yulu the kingfisher and the young man who had just been initiated. These fled in different directions to found new tribes, but the bodies of the Arkaroo serpents are still there and to be seen as the steep encircling walls of Wilpena Pound.

While on the subject of Aboriginal religion, I should mention that among the paintings hung in the state art gallery, I was tremendously moved by a bark painting collected on Groote Eylandt off northern Australia. It depicts the night sky and Orion (as three fishermen trailing their catch of fish) and the Pleiades as their wives in the grass shelter of a women's camp, painted by Minimini. The sheer elegance of placement of the two constellations on an oblong of suitably sombre bark, puts everything I've seen of modern Australian art in the shade. The Adelaide gallery, in fact, owns perhaps the finest collection of Aboriginal paintings, brought south by an American/Australian scientific expedition in 1948.

There is no doubt that the first time you set out to drive into the desert, the awesome distances and emptiness do give you cause for thought. That is part of the pleasure of going. Port Augusta is the ideal take-off point: north to the Simpson Desert or west across the Nullarbor Plain.

The Stuart Highway is now metalled right through to

Darwin. Gone are the days of braving long stretches of corrugated dirt and avoiding treacherous pot-holes. The drive is now simplicity itself. You point your car north and for most of the way you don't even need to steer, the road is so straight and totally flat. For most people there are only three destinations throughout the entire 2750 kilometres: the Coober Pedy opal-mining district; Uluru (Ayer's Rock), 270 kilometres off the highway; and Alice Springs. There are other stops, equipped these days with comfortable motels and service stations, but they are fairly sparse nonetheless.

When I was first in Coober Pedy in 1957 there were only two buildings above ground, the garage and the post office-cum general store. The residents – opal fossickers every one – lived in burrows dug in the stony wastes. Living underground was the only way of coping with the intense summer heat. It was pretty intense in winter too, I can tell you, just as the cold at night was bitter. The opals were (and still are) world famous. The opal-miners were considered either heroic or mad. Since then, things have changed radically. Quite a few residents do still live underground, but they have made roomier quarters for themselves and can procure many standard comforts to furnish them with. The tiny Roman Catholic chapel is still a dug-out. Even one of the new motels offers tourists the experience of underground rooms and suites, though as you may imagine this is simply a short way to kid yourself. The pioneer experience it apes was very primitive and rugged. And the whole motive is missing: the mesmerism of hope. I spent a day, all that long time ago, hunting through the slag-heap tailings and found one small but passable stone, a lovely dark blue, and a dozen chips of white opal (the least valuable kind), but I had to be dragged away by mainforce. I was in the grip of the gamble. The next bucketful of broken stones, the next hour of stunning, addictive boredom would bring me a fortune.

104

Like just about any other real experience there is, you cannot share it through a coach window or with the key to your air-conditioned motel unit safely in your pocket. Adventure is still there – Australia really does offer this – but you must go off the beaten track to find it. You must, I suppose, put yourself at risk, and you must certainly not be worried about petty comforts. I am at the same time saddened and, I must admit, jubilant, when I watch coaches and cars whizzing along the Stuart Highway, knowing they will not stop between the 200-kilometre staging-points: saddened because they are missing the real beauty of the country, the pure air and sublime reaches of space, missing the unique sensation of total aloneness, and the mystery of feeling over-powered by the very featurelessness of the land and its indifference to your being there; but jubilant that its quality of being untouched, its survival even, is more or less guaranteed by this tourist timidity, this obsession with speed and the sticking to a schedule for getting from A to Z.

As an index of how fast the area has witnessed a growth in tourism, I find in my 1957 notebook the record of a conversation with a miner, a single man aged about forty. 'Yes,' he said, 'there's more and more of you city folks come through than ever I recall. You'd be about number twenty, I shouldn't wonder.' This was in August. Last year the information centre at Coober Pedy recorded 90,000 visitors. Naturally, there are now banking services, supermarkets, clubs and even a golf course to divert those 90,000 from the harshness of the place they have come so far to experience.

Travelling north again, you leave behind you the salt lakes with their glittering mirage of non-existent water, the flat, flat terrain speckled with tufts of spiky spinifex grass and the rubble of desolate broken stones around the opal diggings, to a place of jagged rocky hills and outcrops, shrubs and gullies, and you know you are approaching the Northern Territory border.

One last point to make about driving along this road. It is very ill-advised to do so at night; first, because the petrol stations are mainly shut after dark and it will most likely be at least 150 kilometres to the next one (you can thump on the door of the proprietor's flat and get him or her out of bed, but you will be charged a fairly substantial 'wake-up fee' for the privilege; and second, because herds of cattle often wander across it, not to mention kangaroos, and you'd be lucky to see them in time to stop, so seduced by speed does one become on a road as long and featureless as this, its straightness nagging and relentless like a toothache.

Heading west from Port Augusta instead of north, you pass some distinctive granite rock formations at Wudinna and you can call at the sleepy fishing town of Streaky Bay, which has a lot of character and makes a pleasant stop, or press on to Ceduna, the last sizeable town before the Western Australian border. Like Streaky Bay, this is a grain-handling port with great silos at the waterfront as well as a fishing fleet which goes out mainly for whiting. Tuna are also caught right along this coast from Port Lincoln onwards.

Harvesting the sea is a notoriously chancy business, though, especially with large Japanese boats working the area too. Productivity has not kept pace with expectations. But the ailing industry has had a bit of a shot in the arm recently with the development of a new market: sashimi tuna fishing for export (by way of tit for tat) to Japan. I went out on one of the boats to see what happened. This sort of thing is not difficult to arrange as long as you go about it in person. I simply hung about on the wharf, expressing interest, until one boat owner got talking and invited me aboard. I agreed to meet him there early the following morning. We left at three o'clock, the lights on shore bucking wildly as we hit the swell. The skipper headed towards the continental shelf and, sixteen nautical miles out to sea, set about laying his 'long line'. First he was in contact with other fishermen in the area – we could see their lights bobbing ahead and to starboard, then dipping out of sight because the swell was strong, and strong on the stomach too – and I couldn't help wondering where else in the world such a laid-back conversation might take place, considering how chancy a fisherman's livelihood is, how much depends on where he casts. It began with a good deal of laughter and backchat, interspersed with business. 'Where are you shooting your line?' came a voice in a cracked bellow over the radio. 'It makes no difference to me, mate ... north or south, what about you?' (It made a great deal of difference, of course.) Our skipper then explained to me that, since two other boats were there before him, courtesy required that he consult them because they had first choice of where to shoot. You had to respect each other's rights and play by the rules. Even here, I thought, even in this business of butchery, there is room for everyone and time for people not to feel too threatened to show their gentle side. The radio bellowed again: 'Yes, mate, I'm trying to unscramble me brains from last night ... if you remember! ... OK ... well I'm going to shoot along the shelf.' 'Well I'll work inshore of you, all right?' 'No worries.' The skipper told me that since each boat would be shooting a line about 14 kilometres long with maybe 250 branch-lines attached to it, havoc would result from drifting too close and getting them tangled.

If and when the tuna are caught, they have to be handled with extraordinary care if they are to be saleable on the sashimi market. Gone are the old days of poling the fish, throwing them in across the deck to thump and roll into the hold (because for canning purposes a few bruises and wounds make little difference). No, on this boat the three crew

107

members laid out foam mattresses ready for their catch! As they pulled each fish in, they used a rifle to shoot it in the water to prevent it from thrashing about and damaging itself against the gunwale. Then they lifted the magnificent silver body with the greatest care and laid it on the mattresses. This was quite a job, some of these fish weighing 100 kilos.

The technique requires killing a tuna in such a way that the meat will retain the finest possible flavour for eating raw. It is a warm-blooded fish, unlike most, and this is why the catching process is so critical. The skill lies in draining its blood quickly and killing its nervous system which, even after the fish is technically dead, can send emergency signals along the spine generating heat enough to partially cook the meat, thus ruining it. Sashimi fishermen puncture the main blood vessels, surgically remove the brain and thread a wire down the centre of the spine to kill the nerves. Then they cut the pectoral fins off to prevent them bending the corpse which would open the grain of the flesh, slip it into a giant cheesecloth stocking to minimise scratching in the hold, and pack it away in ice. When they get back to port, twelve hours or so after setting out, the tuna are sent by truck to the nearest major town and there packed in dry ice, boxed in cardboard cartons, and flown to Tokyo to be auctioned, generally within forty-eight hours of being alive in the Southern Ocean.

Some tuna are kept for the Australian market, too, because we now have many fine Japanese restaurants in all the main cities. Our relationship to Japan, I might say, has changed radically since they presented us with the fearful threat of invasion during the Second World War, launching air raids against the north (Darwin was bombed fifty-nine times and much of the town lay in ruins), and penetrating into Sydney Harbour with miniature submarines which were depth-charged but not before firing torpedoes aimed at the US

108

cruiser *Chicago* and sinking, instead, a converted ferry filled with sleeping naval ratings.

Far more than the Germans, the Japanese were hated here for their treatment of prisoners of war held in Malaya and as enforced labour on the Burma Railway. But, with trade swinging more and more their way, our growing financial dependence on their markets and their goodwill have gradually brought about a great change. True, their own outward stance has altered beyond recognition and manufactured goods such as Toyota cars and Sanyo television sets are part of our daily life, but it seems not so very long ago, when I was at school in Brisbane, the Japanese were considered subhumanly evil. Even more recent, though less dramatic, has been our change of heart concerning China – not so long ago regarded as the arch-threat to the Pacific region and the source of supposed yellow hordes lusting to sweep down and envelop us, now a friend and partner in many enterprises, study programmes and trade.

Occasionally, one is unfortunate enough to witness a flare-up of residual enmities left over from the past. A particularly embarrassing situation of this kind happened quite recently to my wife and me. We had been asked by the Department of Foreign Affairs to be host to a visiting German professor. I had met him several times when I was overseas as a cultural representative of Australia. He was a most courteous man with flawless English, tall, blond and still youthful at forty-five or so. We took him into a local bar because he wanted to see what it was like. We explained that our bars are not at all comparable to those wonderful German drinking houses redolent of past glories and civilised bonhomie, nor of English pub comfort, the quiet sociability and cosy decor. Australian bars tend to be swill-houses. This is not meant to imply that there are no pleasant bars at all, but that you need to know where you are going because the likelihood is that the atmosphere will be fairly rough and ready. Still, he insisted good-humouredly that he was here to find out about life in Austr-alia, so ... We took him in. Knowing the publican slightly, we introduced our German professor. After a few perfunctory pleasantries, the publican asked the visitor's age and com-mented: 'You'd be too young, then, of course.' 'Too young for what?' 'To bear any of the blame. Nobody was to blame apparently. But you'd be the perfect type. Just what Hitler ordered, blond hair, good-looking, yes you'd have suited him pretty well, I reckon. What are you here for, anyway?' 'He's the guest of our government,' I intervened rather stiffly. 'Oh, that'd be right!' the publican declared with a sneer meant to convey his opinion of governments in general, and excused himself to go and supervise the other bar.

What could be done? We left the beer we had ordered and took our guest to a nearby restaurant where he was received in the friendliest manner and given a wonderful lunch of fresh oysters and avocado. He had carried it off with admir-able aplomb, I must say, but it is no use pretending the ugly incident did not happen.

I thought of Adelaide, not so far away, and the respected German wine-making community. This was a useful reminder that there are no simple generalities and the moment you think you have found one, along will come a surprise experience to knock it for six.

110

6   *The Most Remote of Cities*

PERTH ~ WESTERN AUSTRALIA

Australia Day falls on 26 January, celebrating the establishment of the colony in 1788. The most characteristic
festival, however, is Anzac Day on 25 April, which com-
memorates the landing at Gallipoli, in the First World War.
Throughout the country, dawn services are held in remem-
brance of the dead of all the wars in which Australia has
fought.

With first light pearling the sky, streetlamps dimly glowing
still, waking birds twitter. Feet shuffle toward a memorial
as wreaths are laid and medals clink faintly. The service
culminates with the 'Last Post' and 'Reveille' being sounded
by a lone bugler (an inspired touch, this). The service can
be moving and atmospheric. Later in the morning the same
veterans parade through the streets, accompanied by squads
of servicemen and women, boy scouts, members of the St
John's Ambulance Brigade and all manner of other persons
in uniform. Bands blare, drums beat, and lots of spectators
gather to watch – especially new arrivals in the country, who
are anxious to learn about the society they are soon to become
part of. Such parades traditionally end at 11 a.m. in front of
the cenotaph, where a second service is conducted.

In my view, the truest flavour of Anzac Day is to be found
neither in cities nor tiny outback settlements, but in the
larger country towns. Here, the occasion reveals its most
human aspects – and may also show a comic side as well
when things go wrong. The parade will usually be headed
by a youth leading a horse. He wears his grandfather's Great
War uniform, his slouch hat complete with slightly mould-

111

ering emu feather. The horse he leads is saddled but rider-
less – empty boots strapped back-to-front in the stirrups, as
a symbol for those who did not return. From then on,
precedence is generally allotted by age. I can remember, for
many years, survivors of the Boer War heading the Brisbane
march. Now, even Second World War veterans look grey and
stooped, markedly fewer, and with old faraway faces, stepping
out in Sunday suits, medals bouncing on their chests. The
march ends, and they gather in the open air for the service.
Anzac Day, though heavily dependent on Christian hymns
and appeals to God, is non-sectarian, and even, I think it is
fair to say, basically non-religious. As a rule, the celebrant
will be the president of a local branch of the Returned
Servicemen's League; and the charm of these country
occasions, as distinct from the city observances, is that he
will call on this person or that – dignitaries all – referring to
them as 'Bill' or 'Clarrie' or 'Sister Atkinson' to deliver the
prayer of thanksgiving ('for all great and noble acts, known
and unknown, which we believe by the mercy of God will
bring about the final conquest of forces of evil ...' and so
on), or the prayer for the Queen ('Almighty God ... be
pleased to bestow on her the blessings of Divine Wisdom
...'), or the prayer for the nation ('... that the same com-
radeship and service shown in the last great struggle in which
our country was involved, may now be offered ...').

You can be sure that back in the city there will be some
who murmur sardonically at this, because the last great
struggle was Australia's involvement in Vietnam, among the
most recent of the world's inexcusable wars – and what's
more, we were not only in the wrong, not only fighting an
undeclared war, but we were on the losing side for once; also
there will be a contingent of women quite justifiably angry
at not being permitted to participate in the parade bearing
their banners: WOMEN AGAINST RAPE IN WAR.

112

In country towns such disturbances do not happen. The President of the RSL thanks Jimmy for this and Noel for that, asks the school cadet band to play a number while a collection is taken up, and invites the assembled crowd to give them a round of applause afterwards. The real tragedy is there, without doubt. It is a complex thing, made up of genuine suffering and courage, fear, pain, cowardice, heroism, anger and grief – and memories of a great and terrible adventure, which for many men and women marked their only escape ever from the drudgery of mundane routines.

Although civilian victims are not represented, this is, curiously, a genuine people's celebration. It is a day for participants, not spectators. Akin to a religious procession in this regard, the point is the personal commitment of being there to walk down the middle of the street and be numbered among those making a public demonstration in memory of tragedies big enough to shake whole nations – if not to discredit the profiteers in whose interests these wars are fought.

All afternoon and evening the old soldiers drink beer, till they stagger home, blearily sentimental, having enjoyed a reunion with comrades, swapped yarns about the war (whichever it was) and perhaps also reaffirmed their bewilderment at how their lives, as powerless individuals, are taken over by great and little events alike.

Despite the fact that I, myself, did not fight in any of the wars, that I reject militarism, and despise the rhetoric (above all, the frequently voiced idea that going to war marked this nation's coming-of-age), I cannot escape the power of these occasions, the real human warmth and dignity behind so much that is posturing and pompous.

In Albany, Western Australia, there is a memorial on a headland above the port which can scarcely fail to move an

Australian old enough to remember anything at all of the Second World War. It is a bronze statue originally set up beside the Suez Canal where it remained until toppled during the crisis in 1956 and now re-erected here, at the last home port of departing troop ships. Looking down over the magnificent expanse of King George Sound and back across the stony hills where small splashes of scarlet mark the spectacular flowering of a local species of gum tree, I suddenly knew in a rush of emotion what it must be to see all this with the eyes of those conscripted to fight, knowing it might be for the last time ... and that, for many men and women it was indeed the last time.

Albany, an interesting place and far more inviting than the rather bleak South Australian town of Ceduna at the opposite end of the Great Australian Bight, was once a whaling station. So many early settlements were. This one remained in operation longer than any other in the country. Now, of course, under the international agreement to which we are signatories, whaling is illegal. The station has been turned into a museum. I should think five minutes spent watching harpooning and flensing operations on the documentary film they show here should be enough to convince anyone that the cessation of this butchery was almost as much a blessing to man as it was to the whale.

Nearby, one can walk out to a cliff overlooking the Southern Ocean. The next landmass is Antarctica. And it feels like it. The boulders are massive. Mighty chunks of rock form a bridge under which the waves seethe, while headlands jut out to present the icy swell with granite bluffs. Guard-rails allow the sightseer to lean right over sheer chasms and peer down to where perpendicular rockfaces stand wreathed in delicate veils of mist and the tracery of fleeting waterfalls each time a giant wave sinks down as rushing foam and the boom of its departure heralds the onslaught of

114

another. On the viewing platform, at least 100 metres up, you can be drenched by the spray even on an ordinarily mild day.

Albany was the first town founded in Western Australia and was expected to become the capital of the colony. There's a handsome old residency building still bearing witness to this unfulfilled promise. Twenty years later, in 1848, the charming Church of St John was built. The great harbour and its facilities of a major port stand largely unused now. Big container vessels and tankers no longer need to refuel here, and passenger liners have been superseded by air travel. The town relies more than ever before on the products of surrounding dairy- and sheep-farming districts.

To pick up our journey through Australia, driving or travelling by train into Western Australia from South Australia: this is the most famous of our long dry stretches – the Nullarbor Plain, crossed by the Indian Pacific Railway line and the Eyre Highway.

Between Ceduna, SA, and Norseman, WA, there are two principal places of interest: Eucla and Cocklebiddy. The ghost-town element of Eucla, despite the fact that it is on the highway, is as dramatic as Ravenswood in Queensland (to be described later). But, unlike just about every other case in the country, this was not a mining town where the gold or copper ran out. Eucla was overwhelmed by sand. Huge creeping dunes enveloped the farms and the old telegraph station. The cause was a couple of introduced species of timid animals – the sheep and the rabbit.

Impermanence has marked the whole history of white Australian settlement: after a mere two centuries, the landscape is astonishingly littered with rusted relics of machinery and crumbling, abandoned towns. The greed for short-term profit, whether in mining or agriculture, timber-getting or water-usage, has left Australia with complex problems. Again and again the delicate balance between land use and land abuse has been violated. It still is being violated. The bitter irony is that each time a collapse occurs it is treated as bad luck, or due to over-regulation by government, or some such bogey. Those who take the profit and clear out seldom seem to accept any blame for the ravages they leave behind. This is how native cedar forests were wiped out on the east coast; this is how the banks along the lower reaches of the Murray River are being rendered infertile from rising salinity due to irrigation schemes further upstream; this is how so much of the usable land has eroded back to bedrock and, in the interests of the same shortsightedness, even the Great Barrier Reef is in danger from oil-prospecting companies wanting licences to drill there. Thankfully, we now have an active conservation movement to alert public opinion to such dangers, but the further survival of this land's treasures is still in the balance. Eucla stands as a memorial to folly.

The fact is that no indigenous animal has hooves. This may not at first appear to matter all that much. But the effect of hundreds of millions of sheep, cattle, horses, goats, donkeys, pigs and camels has been absolutely devastating on plants and soil-types which never had to withstand such pounding before. The rabbit, usually named as public pest number one, has probably done no more damage than the sheep; but considerable wealth has been made from wool, so its popular image is very different. Eucla began as a telegraph station, which became one of the busiest in the country. A small township soon grew round it and farmers put sheep out to graze. Then the rabbits moved in. Together, they effectively destroyed the natural ground cover, they bit the vegetation down to the roots and scuffed the roots out. This let loose enormous drifts of sand which crept in to engulf the farmhouses themselves. With the building of the east–west highway, new life came to the town. But the ravages may

116

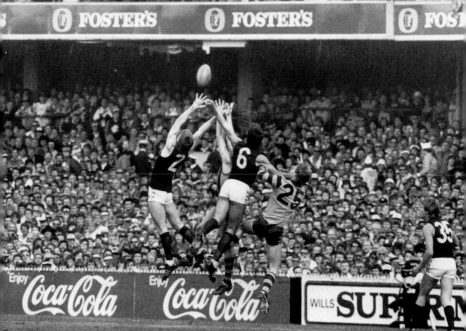

25 Australian Rules Football: Hawthorn beating Carlton at Melbourne Cricket Ground, Sept. 1986; to the uninitiated the game may well seem to be misnamed – the action flows so freely there seems to be no rules at all, Australian or otherwise

26 Aquatic pyrotechnics: professional surfer Ian Cairns in action

27 Wisteria-clad homestead, Glenisla, with the hosts Mr & Mrs Barber (*l*) and a guest. This host farm, built in the 1870s, stands near the rugged Grampians range in Victoria

28 Empty beer cans ring Birdsville Hotel after the town's annual horse race. A classic outback hotel, it lies at the edge of Simpson Desert in the remote west of Queensland

still be seen on the outskirts. From the top of the Eucla Pass you can look back on a stunning view of the white sandy desert you've come through, the desert that is taking over again.

Three hundred kilometres west of Eucla a unique formation begins, though there is nothing on the surface to warn one how unique it is. This is the beginning of the world's largest limestone slab – marginally bigger than France. 'So what?' you may say. 'A limestone slab isn't going to look very interesting.' And it doesn't. It is flat and barren. But at the tiny hamlet of Cocklebiddy (population about 180) there is a strange hole in the ground, an open fissure leading down to water. The local people have all sorts of stories to tell about this mysterious place, but not half so mysterious as the facts have proved to be. The cave follows a fault-line under the surface of the Nullarbor Plain. Basically it is a horizontal cave floor, completely submerged for most of its length, though every so often opening into a chamber where divers can come up for air. And they need it: the total known length of the cave, thought to be the longest in the world and including the world's largest subterranean lake, is almost six kilometres. This passage was explored by a French expedition in 1983 in rivalry with an Australian party the same year. Speleologists now come from all parts to dive here. As there is one stretch of almost two kilometres completely underwater, it is something of an endurance test and has come to be a sort of Mount Everest for caving enthusiasts, who tackle it with modern scuba gear, motorised submarine scooters, and high-powered lights, the actual advance divers needing to be supported by a 'base camp' of speleologists with massive amounts of equipment, all of which costs rather a lot to mount. The French team came with the help of such wealthy sponsors as Mercedes-Benz. To confirm the Everest comparison, the leader of that expedition, M. le Guen, quoted to the press an answer made by Sir Edmund Hillary in 1953, when asked why he climbed the Himalayas, 'Parce qu'elles sont là.'

I should mention that, barren as the land is, there are motels placed every 200 kilometres, or so, right along this road to Albany.

Near the small town of Denmark is a popular spot called the Valley of the Giants. Western Australian tourist publicity will tell you this is where one finds the giant karri and tingle trees, a surviving sample of the grandeur that has been long since cut down elsewhere for logs, or to be cleared as pastures, which an expanding farming community demanded. Don't believe it. The place is tragic. Here and there a mighty tree survives – but only just – its trunk eaten out by repeated fires during the obsessive burning off that has been carried out each year to prevent uncontrolled bushfires. Characteristically, these big trees remain alive only half-way up their trunks ... in fact as far up as the canopy of the newer growth reaches. Beyond that, the leaves have been blown off, the bark has dried and fallen and a colossal skeleton of whitened wood pokes up as bare bones, which the regenerating forest around it will take another hundred years to reach. The forests have been despoiled, and to see these ragged remains is little more than a provocation to anger.

Throughout the country there is a curious aspect to the man on the land. Warm and generous though he may be, deeply knowledgeable about the soil, plants, wildlife and the weather, it is hard to avoid the conclusion that he feels an almost universal hatred against the bush in its wild state. This beautiful land is treated as an enemy by those who live on it. Not until they have wholly destroyed its natural aspect and subjugated it to their service can they love it.

The forests everywhere are in peril. More than 60 per cent of Australian forests have been wiped out altogether in the

118

past century, among them unique native cedar forests in the border areas between New South Wales and Queensland, and the peppermint gum forests of Victoria. The peppermint gum, rivalled only in height by the Californian *Wellingtonia gigantea* has been so decimated that not one specimen of fully mature height is known to survive. At the London Exhibition of 1851, a peppermint gum plank was shown which measured an astounding 44 metres in length, as well as being 50 centimetres wide and 152 millimetres thick. Nine years later another was sent which was 23 metres long and 3 metres broad! The German botanist Baron von Mueller reported finding a living tree 128 metres (420 feet) high, which is higher than the spire of Salisbury Cathedral. None like this survives. No wonder that early in 1987, when scientists discovered a huon pine tree in Tasmania, which modern dating methods calculate as being over 3200 years old and still alive (thought to be the second oldest living organism on earth), they kept its whereabouts a close secret.

The south coast of New South Wales, the west coast of Tasmania and the rainforests in north Queensland, all are being ruthlessly logged, in some cases for nothing better than to be shredded as chips for the Japanese woodchip market where they are sold to paper manufacturers who would not be allowed to touch a single tree of the surviving forests in Japan. Conservationists and woodchippers are in conflict over this issue, which one hopes will be resolved in favour of the trees before it is too late altogether.

People assure me that Perth – the world's remotest city – is vivacious, exciting and beautiful. I have to admit that I find it dull. I returned to the west last year, hoping to encounter the place I still hear reported as being there. For me, it doesn't exist: just a little city, fully absorbed with navel-gazing. Its loyal citizens, obsessed by cleanliness and sunbathing, congratulate one another on living in a place so

119

vivacious, so exciting and so beautiful. On weekdays Perth strikes me as half-dead – and totally dead on Sunday. The location is fine, the Swan River describes a broad sweep around parklands and freeways, which usurp all the most interesting sites. People are friendly, this cannot be denied, and the pace is leisurely. Yet the city seems to have no heart, no shape, no character. In search of character, you should catch the first available train (or taxi, if desperate) to the port of Fremantle.

Fremantle has everything the capital city lacks: heart, vitality and charm. Until a few years ago, it was a run-down wharfside town, left in a state of semi-abandonment by the collapse of the overseas shipping trade. As soon as the great ocean liners of P&O, Sitmar, Lloyd Triestino and the Orient Line no longer called there *en route* for Colombo and the Suez Canal, trade fell away disastrously. Then came rescue from a most unexpected quarter: the Royal Perth Yacht Club's entrant in the America's Cup yacht race beat the Americans. On 11 October 1983, 400,000 people lined the streets to welcome home the victorious crew of *Australia II*.

Almost immediately, plans were drawn up for Fremantle to be host during the 1986 challenge. Not only were the harbour facilities remodelled and new hotels built, but the entire town was given a face-lift. Fremantle, having been ignored as too down-market for developers to bother with, remained wholly free from high-rise towers. This was a complete town still on the human scale. All it needed was cleaning, painting and refurbishing to become one of the most quirkily charming places in the country. Fremantle is the place to drink coffee, buy books, eat out, and simply enjoy strolling.

So much for the towns.

For those who like to rough it, whether you visit the jarrah forests, relatively complete for almost 300 kilometres along the spine of the Darling Scarp to Perth, or go further north to those dry featureless plains which become such a breath-taking mass of spring wildflowers between the months of August and November, or north again to the red sandy desert rich in iron ore and seared by the perpetual heat, you will find camping is allowed.

Three categories of campsite are available: those run by shire councils and providing full facilities for caravans as well as tents; those rather more remote, but still clearly marked, where a car may be parked though nothing more elaborate than water and toilets are provided; and those reachable only by bushwalkers carrying all their basic supplies and equipment in rucksacks. In some national parks and state forests a fee is charged. In others there is a limit on the number of nights you may occupy the one spot.

The rules of camping out are to be extremely careful with fire (the romantic notion of sitting round a blazing log really cannot be done with safety in any forest area); to dispose of all rubbish, either by taking it back out with you or burning and burying it; not to use firearms; and to respect the fact that native flora and fauna are protected by law.

The showplaces for wildflowers are easily reached from Perth and are really not to be missed. Australia is as won-derfully rich in unique plants as in the more celebrated animals; everything from tiny ground covers to large blos-soming trees. And nowhere in the country can outdo Western Australia. The annual carpets of pink, white, yellow and purple, buds like dangling drops of fire, petals the colour of sky and fragile as dragonfly wings, stems like a standing string of blue beads, bushes with silver leaves, with rich yellow blooms, and whole trees blazing scarlet, there can be few places so dull through the rest of the year that boast so great a glory in season.

Apart from seeing the flowers, the two choice areas of the

state – either of which would make the long journey here from the east well worth while, or justify a stop-over if approaching the country across the Indian Ocean – are the Kimberley District and the Pinnacles Desert.

I can comment only from hearsay and from poring over photographs of the Kimberley District. This remote north-western corner of the continent is top of my list for places to go which I have not yet been to. Australia as a whole presents a daunting area to anyone who hopes to see it all. But the Bungle Bungles would definitely seem to be a major attraction. Friends of mine who know them simply rave about the place. These ancient mountains cluster together as little domed peaks, hundreds upon hundreds of them, all bare earth-brown rock, marked right across the range as if by a design artist who has a flair for bold strokes with dark and pale bands of horizontal strata. The effect is quite astonishing. They are apparently wonderful to walk among and look at in the light of different times of day. The access road is rough, though, so you need to travel with one of the outback tour companies, or hire a four-wheel-drive vehicle and make careful inquiries about the state of the road before venturing along it. One gets fairly close to the Bungle Bungles on the Northern Highway between Derby and Wyndham.

There are other attractions in this area including the Wolf Creek Crater, the world's second-largest meteorite hole. It is reached by travelling 146 kilometres out of Hall's Creek along the Tanami Track. Visitors are advised to check with the Hall's Creek shire about the condition of the track before-hand. Nearer Derby is Geikie Gorge, which looks remarkable. The scenery will even withstand the interminable commentary one is traditionally obliged to sit through at friends' slide shows! Tunnel Creek, Windjana Gorge and the adjoining Oscar Ranges are part of what was once an underwater coral reef, folded up above sea-level many millions of years ago and since worn into fascinating shapes. Geikie Gorge is open to visitors in the dry season and three rangers are permanently stationed there. You can take what they call an aquatic tourist coach (a large open motorised punt) and putter round, drifting on the broad calm waters, while a guide steers you in along an overhang of fantastically worn rock. The major rivers of the area have cut through the ranges and laid bare fossils in thick strata, offering a unique cross-section of the remote past. The Fitzroy River, a mighty body of water in the wet season, subsides round about the end of March. By early April the roads have usually dried and become open to traffic. If in doubt, details may be obtained from the State Department of Conservation and Land Management.

As for the Pinnacles Desert, this I do know, and if you have any imagination at all I can assure you that you will find the area absolutely haunting. As far as I understand, there is nothing else like it anywhere. Imagine, in a barren desert of ochre sand, coming upon a landscape of standing rocks about the size of the stones at Avebury or Stonehenge, except that they have been left there by natural causes, which extend as far as the eye can see. A complete forest of them, which was thought at first to be a forest of fossilised tree-stumps. One almost asks: 'What can it *mean?*' These lime-stone pillars and nodules were formed by a most unusual process.

Countless millions of years ago, the sand which had been formed largely of pulverised shells formed into huge dunes which were stabilised by vegetation. The key to the mystery lies in the root systems of the shrubs and trees, which needed to probe deep to reach reliable water, even breaking through cracks in the crust of a calcrete layer under the soil. As a result of climatic changes, the vegetation eventually withered away, rain and wind widened the cracks and loosened the

123

dunes. The sand began moving again. But where the roots had reached down, the chemical changes they brought about gave their enclosed spires of hardened sand a more resistant quality. Through the dry conditions at the height of the last glacial period (during the most recent 25,000 years) these solid cores of rock have remained while the surrounding land crumbled again. The entire formation process took place underground and only appeared on the surface much later.

No one knows quite when this phenomenon became visible. Dutch sailors landing here in 1658 near the site of the present town of Cervantes failed to mention any such thing. So did George Grey's expedition in 1839. Only in the early 1960s did the pinnacles become known. Scientists believe it is quite possible that the wind has uncovered them within the memory of a human lifespan; also, that these pinnacles may not long remain visible before the great shift of sand covers them once more. The knowledge that something so ancient (like the dried bones of Earth itself) could so easily be lost to sight, again within a lifetime, gave me a feeling that this was an especially rare and precious experience, a revelation cosmic in its implications – the sort of place one can imagine other cultures holding sacred: the story being told and retold of how someday the sign of the stones must sink back under an unstoppable drift of time – jagged points, parallel-sided columns, spikes and phallic pillars sinking with majestic slowness back where they had emerged from.

Cervantes is only 180 kilometres from Perth. That 'only' invites further comment. Australians are addicted to the motorcar. The longer the distance that has to be driven, the greater the point in going. From negotiating the suburban traffic in Perth to cross the entire city to buy a favourite kind of icecream, to amateur actors converging once a month on a tiny outback community hall for rehearsals of a musical, some cast members facing a round trip of 1500 kilometres, is a chore we take for granted.

Once when travelling through central Australia, some friends and I came on the boundary huts of a large isolated property at about 5 p.m. Not till 6.30 p.m. and well after dark did we reach the imposing stone structure of the main homestead, only to find it in complete darkness. We needed water rather urgently. Then we spotted some cracks of flickering light showing from behind blinds drawn across the bay windows. Mystified, two of us went to investigate. Peeping in through the cracks, we saw a party of guests watching a film. Home movies. Then we realised we could hear the distant throb of a diesel generator. When we went round the back to knock at a door, there were at least half a dozen light aircraft at the end of the strip beyond the home paddock and a dozen expensive but very dusty cars parked in the yard. The man who answered our knock (very irritably, as it happened) was dressed in a dinner suit complete with black tie and stiff shirt front – out in the middle of nowhere!

The advent of the motorcar during the first years of the century was greeted with prophetic excitement: people, and by that I do not mean only the rich, saw the car as the solution to the dreadful loneliness of a pioneer life. Unlike those countries which had to wait for Henry Ford's lead in production-line manufacture to see the car as other than an extremely expensive and often dangerous toy, Australian country folk saw it as part of their right to space and freedom of movement. As early as 1905, the Dunlop Rubber Company sponsored motorcar reliability trials (in which Australian-made Thompson steam cars competed among the Benzes and Wolseleys and Reos). On that occasion twenty-eight cars took part, driving from Sydney to Melbourne and back, via Ballarat. Five days later, an astonishing nineteen of the cars had reached Sydney, but the organisers could not pick a winner, so the contestants set off up to the Blue Mountains and back. Even after this, there were still six cars with a chance. The excitement was terrific. Newspapers of the day were crammed full of detailed reports on how each car was measuring up. The stakes were high – the sheer stamina and reliability of automobiles able to last for such long journeys over rough stony roads proved that the public intuition was justified – the brand names became, at one stroke, household names. Here lay the answer to alleviating the harshness of life in remote areas. The organisers sent the remaining contestants back to Melbourne again, to make the total round trip 2042 kilometres. Some trial, in 1905.

The motor industry never looked back.

A personal note: I live in the country, though not inland. My wife and I frequently drive to Melbourne to see our two daughters there (700 kilometres each way) or to Sydney to see the third daughter (450 kilometres each way), or to Canberra (300 kilometres each way) simply to see a film or make music or do some shopping.

So, when I describe the Pinnacles Desert as only 180 kilometres from Perth, you must make your own adjustment as to whether you would think of this as a major undertaking or (local style) nothing more than a two-hour drive each way and a pleasant day out.

On these long roads, where settlements are often two or three days' walk apart, motorists understand how vital it is to be able to depend on one another. If you are in trouble and pull over to the side of the road, someone, probably the first car to come along, will stop. The chances are that he or she will have a good idea of how to assist, or at least be willing to drive you to the nearest telephone.

Once, years ago, when out with my family in our old 3-litre Rover, then on its last but glorious legs, we broke down on a country road miles from anywhere, with no other traffic to be seen and dusk already falling. The girls were small and excitable. They wanted to know what I was going to do. 'Well, there's a farmhouse over on that hill,' I said, 'I'll see if they have a phone.' Not only did they have a telephone but they came down to pick up my wife and children. They welcomed us to tea and home-cooked cakes. The farmer looked at the car and found the trouble: the button in the distributor cap had worked its way off-centre and, while spinning, had literally chewed the terminals till they were worn right away; all that remained were little mounds of metal filings at the bottom of the casing, Understandably, he had nothing which might do as a replacement for this electrical part. So, he rang the nearest town and arranged with someone called Steve to come out when he could. We explained that the component was a Lucas and therefore ought to be fairly easily replaced. Steve apparently asked if we were members of the RACWA, or its New South Wales equivalent, the NRMA. At that time, foolishly, we weren't. Never mind, he would come anyway, once he had finished work.

A cold winter wind blew round the hillside and our abandoned car down at the road, but we were fine, sitting in the kitchen near a big wood-burning stove, our elderly hosts simply delighted at having surprise company, the children on their most winning behaviour. The farmer's wife cooked a sturdy meal for us all, expecting to include Steve, as it turned out, who arrived at about seven o'clock. He had a cheerful tale to tell of how he went about finding something to suit the car – an exotic brand in a bush township of 800. A retired bullock-driver in his nineties had then volunteered the wreck of a Wolseley which, when he bought the car new, set the whole district talking as neighbours twitted him for having tickets on himself and being too snobby to speak to them when he got into his imported machine, and so forth.

The distributor cap, once the cobwebs were cleared away, turned out to be in good order – a Lucas.

Steve presented it in triumph and sat it on the linoleum-covered kitchen table to be admired while we tucked into a meal recalling the age of giants and titans. He had also thought to bring a couple of bottles of beer, as it turned out, in case the job took a while and needed a steady hand. We consumed this, likewise, the girls being treated to thimblesful also. After a laconic discussion of the drought as 'being a bit short on rain in the region,' about scandals said to involve the American president of the time, about sandyblight in the pioneering days, and about the likely premiers in the Sydney rugby football league, the farmer, Steve and I hoisted ourselves up from the table, reluctantly put the comforts of the kitchen behind us, went out into the cold night to the mechanic's battered four-wheel-drive vehicle and down to my stranded old Rover. We talked a lot and joked a lot. Steve switched the caps over – not quite the same but near enough to keep us going at least till we could get the correct part. In answer to my question, he explained that he was the mechanic at a small garage. But no, he said quite cheerfully, he had not had the benefit of any training of any kind whatever, he had picked it up. He grinned at me, one of those sly, generous, mocking, compassionate glances that sees through you immediately; because by now this didn't bother me in the slightest. Apparently I passed the test. The smile became plain matey. We turned the motor over – and she worked.

The farmer's wife wrapped slices of cake for the girls and an apple apiece for us all and asked us to keep in touch. The farmer came back down to the road to watch us safely on our way, and we saw his torch waver back up the hill in the dark. Steve, in the most offhand manner, said 'See how she goes.' and waited while we pulled out. I drove cautiously. Indeed, I slowed down to allow him to pass. But he did not pass.

128

That's how we went, all the way to the town some 40 kilometres along the road. And then, as if we couldn't have realised he was watching over us in case we broke down again, he tooted his horn and turned off home. Only that night did it occur to me that I had so enjoyed being with these friendly people that I'd completely forgotten to pay him.

Next morning we went back. The garage was not hard to find, being the only one. He refused any payment. 'I was getting a bit bored as it was,' he explained, 'when the call came. Good excuse for a breath of fresh air. But,' he added, 'old Vince mightn't say no to a dozen bottles or so.' We duly presented the old fellow with a case of beer. He protested that there was no need and that he could only bring himself to accept if we sat down and cracked the first one with him to celebrate his old bomb out the back which still had its uses.

This was, all in all, a typically Australian occasion.

One of the extraordinary sights of the far north-west is the Wandjina paintings. In most parts of Australia the original creation myths centre on a giant serpent, often a rainbow serpent, and always associated with water, despite his many forms and many names. But in the Kimberley district, over and above the many snakes depicted, there looms Wandjina. Wandjina is far more like the kind of god-figure we are familiar with – creator of earth and sea, of man and woman, giver of the law, a presence both fertile and punitive. The race of people he created took his name and their descendants painted bold images of the ancestor spirits on cave walls: big looming heads with round black eyes and what look remarkably like haloes in medieval art. Some of these timeless images are ritually renewed with fresh ochre and coloured clay pigments.

Though the stories which have been recorded vary considerably from place to place, they share the common basis of naming the owl as Wandjina's totem. When the explorer George Grey came upon these paintings in 1837 he noted in his journal the surprise he felt 'at the moment that I first saw this gigantic head and upper part of a body bending over and staring down at me.' Quite a few such sites may be visited, but they are now strictly regulated and protected by law.

There are five principal categories of Aboriginal painting which may be characterised by what they are painted *on*: those painted on cave walls or cliffs; on portable objects including sheets of bark; on carvings; on the land (including sand paintings); and on bodies. I am not qualified to discuss the implications of these various kinds of painting or their ritual significance, but for the visitor who wishes to seek them out I may make the following general points.

The cave paintings are often quite old, some even ancient, not usually spectacular and frequently in places rather difficult to reach – such as crawling into a mere slit of a cave and craning your neck while you shine a torch on the roof above you – but all the more moving for that and having the inestimable value of being seen necessarily in the particular landscape where they belong. Sand and body paintings are transitory; however long they take to do and however lovingly executed, they are fleeting forms. Again, this very fact gives them a special quality, spoilt only if we insist on taking photographs or movies to fix them and possess their images more permanently. My own view is that to photograph them is to miss the point, quite simply to make it impossible to respond fully enough at the moment to get the most out of it. Nearly all carvings are sacred objects and taboo to outsiders, so these are not often encountered. Many of the carved and painted portable objects were also sacred but found their way – often by genteel theft – into anthropologists' collections and thence to museums.

The most common form of native art is the bark painting. These flat slabs of dried bark are conveniently shaped for transporting and hanging on walls. They are also light to carry. Hundreds of them are to be found in gallery collections right throughout Australia and abroad, and in many places may be bought, often from the artist in person. For this last category, perhaps the best place to visit is the Northern Territory.

7 A Glimpse of the Beginnings of the World

THE NORTHERN TERRITORY

A good deal of fear is generated in the press concerning deadly creatures, especially in the tropical areas. On this subject, let me say that the bush is, in general, perfectly safe. Naturally, there are places where you will need to take simple precautions, such as wearing something on your feet and making sure you have some idea of what to do in case of emergency, but Australia is not like Africa or South America (or even parts of North America) with large dangerous animals roaming the scrub. The only large animals to pose any threat to man – apart from the possibility of a wild buffalo in the far north or a wild pig (neither of them native creatures) – are both found in water: sharks and crocodiles. Crocodile attacks, though sensational, have been very few; and shark fatalities since records began in 1788 average about two people per year, whereas thousands die annually on the roads.

The following summary gives an idea of how to recognise dangerous creatures and what to do about them. But it is not meant to imply that the visitor is at all likely to encounter any one of them. In my time I have seen quite a few snakes, a few poisonous spiders and the occasional dangerous jelly-fish, but neither I nor my family, nor any of my friends has ever been attacked or bitten.

To begin the catalogue at the small end of the scale, there are several kinds of spiders to beware of. The red-back is a rather racy little spider with an unmistakably clear vermilion stripe along its back. Avoid it. A more serious threat is the funnel-web spider, a fat black hairy specimen which is

132

29 Surf-boat competing in a race. These boats are purely for sport nowadays, modern motor-launches being used for surf rescue operations

30 Rams Head Range in the Snowy Mountains on the border of Victoria and New South Wales

31 One of the multiple-
domed peaks of the
Olgas in the Ayers
Rock/Mount Olga
National Park,
Northern Territory.
This mountain rises
500 metres straight
off the plain

32 The Glasshouse Mountains – worn remnants of volcanic plugs – with gum
trees in the foreground, near Brisbane, Queensland

aggressive, one of the few poisonous creatures in Australia to go for you if provoked. They are not commonly seen and shouldn't be confused with the misnamed tarantula, a harmless huntsman spider. The bite of the funnel-web is extremely painful and can be fatal if not treated. It must be handled the same as a snake-bite – that is to say, bind the wound in a crêpe bandage (or equivalent) as if for a sprain, the bandage being firm but not constricting; then immobilise the limb or affected part. The patient needs to remain as inert as possible, and taken to the nearest hospital. Hospitals throughout Australia have a range of antivenenes and sophisticated techniques for identifying poisoned bites.

As for snakes, some are venomous, but almost all are shy. The best protection is alertness. If you see a snake, keep clear of it and it will keep clear of you. People who attack snakes are taking a great and unnecessary risk. Even after being bitten, the victim is advised to let the snake go, to avoid being bitten twice.

Again, the risk must not be over-dramatised. With wider public knowledge of the simple treatment described above, snake-bite fatalities have been reduced from around fourteen persons a year to one. The main thing is to forget the old idea of cutting open the bite and trying to suck out the poison. Just bandage the area, keep it still, and find the nearest hospital.

So much for the dangers of the land. The dangers of the sea are rather more problematical because you have much less chance of seeing them coming.

Perhaps the most venomous of all creatures anywhere is a delicate-looking jellyfish (*Chironex fleckeri*), known as the box jellyfish, and occurring along the northern tropical coast. This small white animal, swathed in a see-through, milky outer-mantle and trailing frail tentacles like harmless white ribbons, is deadly. If stung, rule number one is, as always, 'don't panic'. The treatment is simplicity itself. Flood the wound with vinegar, ordinary household vinegar. This kills the stinging cells. The same applies to the far commoner – and fortunately far less poisonous – Portuguese man-o'-war, a small blue jellyfish found right round the coast. Just as you should wear good stout shoes in the bush, or sandshoes on the rocks and in rockpools, so you should be aware that if a strong sea-breeze is blowing, the danger of bluebottles (as these jellyfish are usually called) is greatly increased because they float on the surface and the wind drives them ashore.

There are two other sea creatures to beware of: the stone-fish and the blue-ringed octopus. Stone-fish are utterly passive. You get stung only if you tread on them, they don't set out to sting you. They are to be found in places such as Moreton Bay (Brisbane) where the salt water is shallow and generally still, and the bottom is muddy. You need have no fear of them at the beach. The protection is to wear something on your feet. The blue-ringed octopus is a gorgeous little chap, quite rare (I have never seen one in the wild), but known to enjoy swimming in rock pools. The bite is near-painless at first, but within minutes affects breathing. The venom is serious. The treatment is the same as for snake-bite, as well as mouth-to-mouth resuscitation.

The simple rule is this: if you go into the bush or swim in the sea, make sure you pack as part of your essential picnic a bottle of vinegar and a crêpe bandage. It is not much, and no more difficult than remembering a tube of suntan lotion.

So, to the carnivores, the sharks and crocodiles.

Sharks, actually, are not very keen on human flesh. In most cases, the shark's first bite is simply a tasting, and after one sample, he probably won't come back. Mind you, that sample can be a whole limb. The sensible precautions are to swim at city beaches between the flags set up on the sand. These areas are patrolled and lifesavers keep watch from

134

their towers. If sharks are sighted (and again, may I say, as an avid beach-lover, I have never been present at a shark alarm) swimmers are advised to leave the water as quickly and calmly as possible.

The crocodile, alas, *does* seem to have a taste for human flesh. Crocodiles are found only in the far north of the country where very few tourists or travelling Australians ever go. But if you do visit these parts, don't swim there. It's as simple as that. Keep a watch out on the banks of rivers and avoid taking risks. Crocodiles are, after all, very large creatures and not hard to see. For the recent upsurge of publicity about them, one must thank the entertainment industry.

The dominant image of Australia abroad – as a country of kangaroos, rough men and hard drinkers, hot inhospitable desert and flies – is periodically trotted out for some money-making venture or other. The latest boost to this image came in the form of an affectionately romanticised version of life in the far north, Peter Faiman's film *Crocodile Dundee*. The cheerful, swashbuckling Dundee, his Aboriginal friend consulting a watch and sulking off to a corroboree when he'd rather be part of the modern world of the whites, the beautiful American reporter lured by tales of a last frontier, all this is harmless enough. But any visitor expecting to walk into that scene had better find out where the next film set is being built.

Behind *Crocodile Dundee*, however, lies a world of considerable interest. The script appears to have been developed from a real-life incident published as *To Fight the Wild*, in which Rod Ansell tells the story of his survival for nearly two months, after a fishing accident in which his boat was lost. His account is modest, astounding and utterly convincing. A young man of somewhat slight build, shy, bookish in his tastes, yet an absolutely professional bushman, makes plain that the kind of country he lived off would kill anyone without

135

the skill and resilience to handle it. One other factor which can never be conveyed by a visual medium such as film is the sensation of isolation. The more you show it on a screen, the more you domesticate it. I cannot too strongly emphasise that the Top End, as it is called, beautiful, alive with birds and marsupials, as well as snakes and crocodiles, is to be approached with some caution. The foreign visitor is well advised to arrange everything through a reliable travel agency.

The odd thing about the *Crocodile Dundee* syndrome is that, healthy and harmless good fun as it is, the reality makes so much better a story. And if the media in Britain are bad enough (with some notable exceptions), the media in Australia are worse. The fundamental practice of vulgarising everything by reducing it to almost Disney-like unreality takes a country which is fascinating and reduces what is bizarre or moving to the quaint and sentimental.

It is well worth a visit 'in the flesh'. During recent years there has been a major push to promote tourism across the Top End – from Broome in Western Australia to Darwin in the Northern Territory. To many Australians, I'm sure, the whole prospect seems unlikely in the extreme. But a great deal of work has been done on the area's accessibility, especially by way of providing for accommodation. The lush tropical vegetation, superb fishing in the Victoria River, the warm thermal pool at Mataranka and the Cutta Cutta Caves are all attractions for the adventurous traveller looking for something different.

Near Katherine, where the Victoria Highway joins the Stuart Highway (the road to Alice Springs, if you are to approach from the north), the gorge is a favourite spot for visitors. Sheer cliffs drop straight into the calm waters. The propaganda has much to say about the breathtaking colour of the rocks, and so forth, but I think this is overdone. It is a lovely place and quite impressive, but not breathtaking. And for truly astonishing colour in the landscape, one should travel 1000 kilometres further south. Katherine Gorge is best viewed from one of the little service boats that ply their trade daily. This can be combined with a call at Springvale, the oldest station homestead in the territory. Springvale has been converted to a tourist park used by many visitors as a base for visiting the almost virgin country out to Roper River. This is *Crocodile Dundee* country and pretty rugged. Anyone exploring these parts would be well advised to check with locals about the kind of vehicles and equipment to take, the weather conditions and the safety precautions to observe while swimming.

I am somewhat sceptical about the Aboriginal corroboree advertised as being at Springvale. My impression is that this might be about on a par, as regards authenticity, with hula dancing at a Waikiki hotel. The true corroboree is either sacred (in which case you would not be allowed to see it even if you were in the area) or the spontaneous celebration of a day's hunting. It is not a prescribed dance-form which can be turned on at the drop of a hat (or coin) with a nod to convention in the patterns of body paint and an even more respectful nod to white prudery in the wearing of colour-coordinated loincloths. I should point out, in passing, that throughout most parts of Australia, the Aborigines did not wear any clothes except occasionally furs in winter in the colder regions. Anyway, I suppose authenticity is not essential in everyone's eyes. It just happens to be that way for me. I have been privileged in seeing, once and once only, some real tribal dancing. It was so subtle and delicate, so refined in its every gesture, that I really do not want to see any vulgarised versions from which the real expressive power has been shed in the deadly repetition of art as a commodity, a curiosity.

The next stage of this journey takes you into a world altogether more startling and impressive.

One of the glories of the Territory is the recently declared Kakadu National Park: an unforgettable experience for the nature-lover. Six thousand square kilometres in area, the park was accepted for registration on the World Heritage List in 1980. The rich vegetation abounds in wildlife. The birds are simply unbelievable: over one hundred species, including the gorgeous wompoo pigeon, rosellas, and flocks of parrots, the air loud with their clamour; and along the flood plains and paperbark lagoons at the northern end vast gatherings of waterbirds, notably jabiru and a magnificent black and white goose known as the magpie goose. Large lustrous insects, reptiles and marsupials are also common, not to mention the glorious scenery including several splendid waterfalls, Jim Jim Falls and Twin Falls. Good camping is available along the Alligator River (incidentally, Australia has no alligators, this is a misnomer ... only crocodiles).

Perhaps the best way to arrive is by air to Oenpelli, then by road to Jabiru – a uranium-mining town named after the bird, which is a large black-necked stork. Using Jabiru as a base a couple of marvellous trips can be planned, quite accessible within a day's return journey. First to the lagoons by paddleboat: a magic country of whispering waters and slender trees. The guides here are knowledgeable bushmen and not at all hectoring or intrusive. Their respect for the place is fine and, thank goodness, the horror of piped music hasn't yet struck. The other 'must' is a walk up Obiri Rock. This is quite a leisurely climb, past caves simply crusted with Aboriginal carvings and paintings. The rock itself is like nothing so much as a sort of Angkor Wat, the strata are laid horizontally and etched deeper by weathering so that it seems almost to have been *built*, brought in from elsewhere, carried to the spot slab by slab and built with devotional zeal count-

138

less centuries ago, then left to rot and crumble. From the top, one is presented with an experience almost as grand as from Uluru (Ayer's Rock). The view looks out over lagoons and flatlands with the ocean on the horizon and two great rivers, one on either side, snaking towards it. I can describe the impression of the scene as nothing less than being haunted by primeval memories, as if present at the burgeoning innocence of the world when first consciously looked upon by human beings. Great clouds gather and sweep inland, disperse and are gone without shedding a drop of rain, for this is the wrong season. Cloud-shadows animate and darken the rich vegetation, the cry of countless birds and the hum of insects only seem to deepen the peace of the place. For sheer power, this landscape is hard to match. What I have described is a scene in September during the build-up to the Wet. There are two seasons in the tropics: the Wet and the Dry. I suspect the most wonderful time to visit Kakadu would be just after the Wet (in March, say) when the floodwaters have drained away and fresh growth is everywhere.

For Australians there is also a unique experience of another kind to be found at Kakadu – a border. Our state boundaries are a joke; administrative lines ruled on maps. Yet here, when you come to the bank of the Alligator River, the water forms a boundary of another kind. Not only the unfamiliar danger of crocodiles – anywhere else in Australia your impulse would be to jump in for a refreshing swim – but knowing that the other bank is the beginning of an Aboriginal reserve which you need permission to enter. It is a curious sensation. In that moment you are brought up sharply against the realisation of how much like an island the whole continent does feel, how we treat it as an island too, with the sea as its only border.

The native diet in Arnhem Land is rich and nutritious though not always easy to find: the meat of the goanna (a lizard growing up to $2-2\frac{1}{2}$ metres in length) is much prized, wallaby and kangaroo, pelican, swan and wild goose, crab, fish, mussels, lily stems, pandanus palm kernels and cycad nuts. The spear had been the main hunting weapon traditionally, but its supremacy is being challenged by the shotgun. The people here still have their tribal skills and much of the old tribal social structure as well.

In 1963, after the successful annexation of what had been their reserve land by transnational mining companies, the Yirrkala people took a petition to Canberra. They wrote in the Gumatj language on a slab of bark and presented it to Federal Parliament. The matter was taken up, but they lost their case in the supreme court on the grounds that Aborigines had no legal title to the land. They did not give in, though their sacred land had been already virtually wiped out by open-cut bauxite mining. Three years later, the fight was taken up again, this time by Gurindji stockmen working the cattle on Wave Hill Station owned by the London-based Vestey group. The stockmen walked off and set up their own outstation at Wattie Creek. They petitioned the Governor-General. It took another nine years and the accession to power of a Labor government for them to win through, but in 1975 the then Prime Minister, Gough Whitlam, went to Wave Hill for a ceremonial handing back of the land to the tribal elders. This historic occasion became the first successful land rights claim by Aborigines. The process of seeking justice elsewhere still goes on.

The point is that the Northern Territory, though it has its own House of Representatives, is still only a Territory and not a full State, which means it comes under the direct authority of the Commonwealth Parliament in Canberra. Since 1972, the Commonwealth Parliament has adopted far more advanced and enlightened racial policies than those States in which most Aborigines live: Queensland, Western Australia, and the Northern Territory. The attitude of the

140

general public – hard enough to assess at any time – is not by any means simple. Certainly, there is plenty of bigotry around, certainly one hears discriminatory opinions too often to be complacent about them. But, in the long term, I still find myself hopeful.

Whatever else may be lacking in Australian society, one thing is certain, the distinctive generosity of spirit in the old-style knock-about bush Australian, who was the national stereotype when I was at school, still lives on in the totally reshaped society we enjoy today. An enormously complex racial mixture has occurred from the migration schemes and from willingly opening the door to refugees from Europe, Asia and South America. With the least possible fuss and friction, these people have found a place here, in some cases a sanctuary. If only we could do as well in accommodating our own Aborigines with their superior rights to belonging, we'd achieve something quite exceptional. Perhaps that will come now that many thinking people acknowledge a debt long unpaid. It could still happen. And this, also, says a good deal about Australian society, which is not by any means closed or self-defensive. There is still that warmth which gives us hope we won't lose what we have achieved and that we will solve the most outstanding anomaly – the refusal to grant land rights to the original owners, who fought a long, heroic, desperate war to stop us taking over and have never surrendered despite the humiliation and penury of the conditions in which most of them live. Personally, I think it will happen. I think there is enough enduring fairness and tolerance to survive this challenge and even grow from it.

Some of Arnhem Land is lush tropical country, hot and damp, green and fragrant, but some is bushland so frail in appearance it is hard to imagine how the sparse, slender saplings, the occasional treefern or palm can yield enough game and seed to sustain people.

And more and more families are going back to live in the wild. Since the granting of title to large tracts of land (even though mining and development companies still enjoy over-riding rights within the law) more than 3000 people have left the settlements, missions and reserves set up for them by whites and have returned to their old way of life. This has proved tremendously beneficial in matters of health, morale and personal happiness. Many of the men still travel to the cattle stations to work as stockmen. But a significant financial benefit is also accruing from their determination not to let their culture die: something like 17 per cent of the income for the whole of Arnhem Land comes from the sale of traditional bark paintings and artefacts.

A recent exhibition at the Australian National Gallery in Canberra showed something of the astonishing range and richness of these Arnhem Land paintings, from arcadian scenes of spirit people and animals in a fruitful land to abstract designs as complex as lace. The fluency and liberty from the kinds of critical concept which dominate western art give these bark paintings the appearance of spontaneous inventiveness.

One of the great painters is Bulun Bulun – unknown, I might say, to the vast majority of Australian art lovers. There is a wonderfully alive account of how he works in Penny Tweedie's book *This Is My Country*, first walking into the bush with an axe and selecting the bark to be cut, then bringing it back into camp to be cleaned and prepared. 'He used a bush knife to scrape it smooth as canvas, then with the aid of fire – the Aborigines' most valuable tool – he straightened the bark and flattened it under a pile of logs.... The children gathered round, squatting in the shade to watch the master at work.' The four colours used in the area are all natural: white from pipeclay and chalk, black from charcoal, red and yellow from the ochres found there, and a fixative made from wild orchid roots. ' "First I cover all the bark with red ochre," Bulun Bulun explained, fumbling in his dilly bag. "You'd better not film this one," he laughed, extracting an old shaving brush and dipping it into the paint.' Having primed the bark, he left it to dry. ' "Now I show you proper Yolngu brush," he said. Shredding some fine strands of bark fibre with a knife he bound them into a stick then dipped his new brush in the yellow ochre and with a bold and steady hand drew a circle in the centre of the bark. "This is a waterhole," he said, explaining that water is the source of all life. Meticulously he outlined the symbols for springs and watercourses and drew his totems: turtles, geese, snakes and flying foxes (a fruit bat).' As he worked he explained what the painting meant – not just to Penny Tweedie, but so that his own children would learn about their ancestry and their country too.

The symbols in this northern art are clearly recognisable and quite unlike the Papunya style near the southern border of the Northern Territory. Papunya is a settlement on the Haast's Bluff Reserve in the Macdonnell Ranges, 200 kilometres west of Alice Springs. Magnificent country, this, but visitors are not encouraged, and special permission must be obtained to enter the reserve. The Papunya paintings are characteristically records of great journeys. They are as completely abstract and inscrutable as classical Islamic art, a rhythmic puzzle of interlocking circles and a maze of interconnections. The paintings are entirely built of dots, usually white on a varying ground of brown and ochre. Decoratively they are beautiful objects, but the tale they tell requires initiation into an elaborate folklore.

Many painters have branched out to produce European-style watercolours which are readily available in Alice Springs. The greatest and most tragic of them was Albert Namatjira who died twenty years ago. He brought to this

143

rather pallid medium a riotous freshness. Many people think his ranges of clear blue mountains on one side and amethyst mountains on the other, the orange-red sand and silver-green bushes, the bright yellow tufts of grass and dark brown rocks are fanciful and imagined. But one only needs to visit that part of the country to find that, if anything, his rendering is gentle and discreet. There can be few landscapes in the world more vivid than this.

Darwin is dull by contrast with the glories of the land to the south, and of Kakadu National Park. What can one say? If you find you have a taste for knockabout, straight-from-the-shoulder Aussie manners, a healthy earthiness and complete lack of ceremony, life lived in a pair of shorts, a skimpy shirt and thongs, plentiful quantities of icy beer, sweltering nights, raucous music and loud laughter, Darwin is for you. If not, there's an awful lot that you'll find tiresome.

Still, the modernising process, for what that brings, has been amazingly swift and sweeping. There are now excellent sporting facilities; also a concert hall, equipped with a superb Steinway grand piano. The Diamond Beach Casino, housed in a sleek bunker of a building, is managed by a team who pride themselves on their links with Aspinalls in London and Sands in Atlantic City. The casino offers the usual range of gambling lures, as well as full hotel accommodation.

The wealth of the new Darwin – it was almost completely flattened by a cyclone in 1974 – is based on the territory's rich mining industries. The tourist season for Darwin and surrounding areas is not governed by temperature as in most other places (the variation being only about 15° between, roughly, 25°C to 40°C) but by the need to avoid the rain which falls torrentially during the summer months.

The only other large town in the Northern Territory is Alice Springs, which was founded in 1872 as a repeater station on the Overland Telegraph Line which linked Australia with the rest of the world, the cable being laid from what was then the Dutch East Indies (Indonesia) to Darwin and then strung across the country to Port Augusta in the south, and on to Adelaide. The original telegraph station may still be seen, a sprawling stone building with wide verandas. Alice Springs has long since outgrown this simple utilitarian function. It is now the setting-out point for the hundreds of thousands of visitors each year who venture into central Australia, to Uluru (Ayer's Rock), the Mount Olga group, to the deep golden corridor of Standley Chasm, the jagged blue hills of Haast's Bluff, the endless quilted foothills of the Macdonnell Ranges, and the extraordinary formations of the vast Finke River bed. The Finke is a river as wide as the Nile, and winding through hundreds of miles of desert country, its high banks cut sharply in the rock, but with just one difference – it is empty of water. You could walk the entire length of the river and find no more than a couple of isolated pools here and there. It is an eerie feeling because the shape of the river is always so clearly to be seen all round you. Curious that, since time immemorial, the river evidently flowed strongly, by its deeply etched course, and that now, so recently in its history and perhaps only as a brief hiatus, there should be no rain in these regions to feed it any longer.

The beauty and variety of the country round 'The Alice' is inexhaustible. I'd recommend anyone to go during the winter months, June to August. Though the nights are crisp and can even be frosty, the days are glorious. The colours in the landscape are beyond imagining: rocks and sand of brilliant orange, red, ochre, a deep blue sky over deeper blue mountains, silver-green shrubs and golden tufts of prickly grass, trees with chalk-white trunks and, after a rare rain-shower, carpets of wild flowers as far as the eye can see. The mountains, including Uluru and the Olgas, are worn smooth and rounded as the fat flanks and hard skulls of colossal half-buried creatures. This extraordinary region is not to be missed.

But what of Alice itself? A local resident summed it up this way: 'The town has two industries – tourism and swallowing the Aboriginal dollar. There are a lot of Aborigines here and other people begrudge them the small government grant moneys they receive, but these same people are often the ones who get hold of that money the moment it's to hand; retailers and publicans. Aborigines love consumer goods, cars, baby clothes and toys, country-and-western gear, checked shirts, riding boots, big hats, wide belts and heaps of food. Not to mention needing car parts, tyres and petrol. When they get their money – wages or social security payments or whatever – they spend it.' I asked about the rest of the community. 'Well, one thing you find. There's one rule. As soon as you've made friends with someone, they move on. The whole territory is like that. A floating population, here for the money and experience, the adventure of trying their luck in the far outback. They stay a while. Then they go home where they've come from, to Adelaide or Melbourne or Sydney, to Woop Woop or wherever. Three years, maybe five, and they're gone. The Americans are even more on the move. They come to work here, maybe four or five thousand at any one time, employed by the Pine Gap outerspace tracking centre ... well, outerspace tracking, for what it's worth ... we don't know *what* they do there. Nobody in Australia does, not even the Prime Minister knows. Top secret. The Americans are a law to themselves. They live in the town with their families, very quietly. Very willing to please and fit in. No fuss. But you can't mention their work. They clam up. There are heaps of bases in this country and we don't know what they are doing here. So here, as you can imagine, some of us who are locals feel bloody strongly about it. Things may seem peaceful on the surface, but they're

146

bubbling underneath, out of sight. Meanwhile, at the level of dollars and cents, the Americans bring trade, even if they cost us a fair bit with our state schools full of their children and so on. The parents, well, my wife and I have had them for neighbours off and on, we've still got two families across the road ... they're polite, faceless. Impact: nil. But I'll tell you this, aside from their groceries, they live off the giant Galaxy transport planes that fly in once a week bringing everything else they need direct from the USA. As for the Aussies, the rest of the population of Alice – well, we're not much to crow about either. Mostly we're nobodies who come from nowhere, we're going nowhere, we've got nothing, and there's nothing we want to know.' He laughed, partly joking, partly sad, and certainly bitter, but just as certainly free and able to shift elsewhere when it suits him.

To the visitor, such a summary does seem rather harsh. Appearances are notoriously deceptive. But Alice Springs, since the advent of air-conditioning, has become much like anywhere else with that anonymous, slightly antiseptic cleanliness and comfort, though admittedly giving the impression that even the buildings are flimsy and somehow temporary. The new cultural centre opens all sorts of possibilities and allows a whole range of visiting artists to include the town on their outback itineraries. Anyway, from the visitor's point of view all modern conveniences are laid on, with a tour company round just about every corner and no shortage of suggestions as to how you might spend your time and your money. My own feeling about Alice Springs is that the sooner I can get out into the desert (having been very grateful to use it as a provisioning base) the happier I am. Not because I feel any dislike of the town but simply because it is so ordinary a place to be in the middle of such a colossal jewel of a setting.

One last comment on possible contact with Aborigines for

those who are specially interested. Beginning in 1988, a new concept in holidays is to be tried out. Australian Kakadu Tours are offering a three-day visit to Melville Island off the coast near Darwin. The holiday is spent among the Tiwi people. Visitors are not only shown how the local people of the land live, but will live that life with them, helping to catch food and cook it in the embers of a campfire, roughing it, and even taking part in dances and so forth. This is a unique experiment. At $700 for three days, as rates go at the time of writing this (July 1987), you would need to be seriously interested to be tempted in the first place. The island is tropical but thanks to its breezes remains always benign, in marked contrast to the steamy heat of Darwin. And the people are hospitable. My guess is if they can continue to welcome visitors as guests rather than seeing them as tourists to be either exploited or wooed, the simple arrangements of tent accommodation and outdoor eating will provide a really memorable experience in a magnificent setting for those attracted to take it up.

8 'She'll be right, mate!'

The Barkly Highway links the Northern Territory with Queensland. It reaches the coast at Townsville – an ideal place from which to begin exploring the Great Barrier Reef. But just before getting there, the road passes through Charters Towers. I made a valiant effort to follow my own advice and combat the motorist's dreadful obsession with pressing on, regardless. I am very glad I did.

The first gold was dug at Charters Towers in 1871. For the next thirty-five years, the diggers rushed there and extracted huge quantities of the precious metal, mainly by panning, which is to say washing the grains of gold free from mud and gravel. Typical of such boom towns, these residents of Charters Towers became extravagantly partisan and boastful about the place: during their most productive years they referred to the local stock exchange as 'The World'. Today one finds a quiet little place. In the main street there's a public bench bearing a plaque to explain that it was donated by the Charters Towers Goat Club.

I drove in on a Saturday afternoon. Though it's a well-known fact that all country towns close down at lunchtime on Saturdays, this one seemed more than usually silent. I wandered along hot streets, hearing my solitary footfalls echoed by empty buildings ... until I spotted a poster which explained everything. By pure chance I had arrived on the day of the Charters Towers Show.

Now I am a man who relishes agricultural shows. I don't know a Hereford from an Aberdeen Angus; and as a gardener I have so deadly a black thumb I can't even grow mint, but

149

I never seem to get enough of wandering among prize-winning horses and cattle; admiring competition vegetables and roses; peering at entries in the needlecraft and cooking sections; acknowledging a touching deference to culture evident in the clumsy art display; watching children buying the same sort of manufacturers' sample bags of sweets and cheap comics I used to lust after as a boy; wandering among the fairground attractions, listening to raucous voices shouting the ticket prices for their dizzy allurements; mingling with the constant to and fro of young women, in jodhpurs and hacking jackets, who slap their high boots with riding crops; young stockmen in their best working clothes perched on the sliprail fences, waiting for their turn to compete in the rodeo; turning now and again to watch the women shyly or slyly, or smoking a quiet cigarette and discussing the grand parade. Pure magic.

This was a small show, based firmly on competitions of work skills. I had a thoroughly enjoyable day watching sheepdog trials and camp-drafting (a mounted stockman cutting his beast out from among the mob and driving it round a course of pegs and out through a 'gate' which was simply two sapling stakes driven into the ground). I enjoyed overhearing country conversations, the laconic casualness of manner, the humour, the festive quality of this folk gathering, so unselfconscious and yet so important in their lives.

I stayed the night at Charters Towers and set off along the highway next morning, taking the turn to Ravenswood, which I knew to be a famous ghost town.

The Ravenswood road is crude and bumpy, but well worth the detour. Gold was discovered here two years before the larger field at Charters Towers. In a very Australian way – a kind of tragic romance of fortitude and capriciousness – the whole history of this living town from its birth to its death was compassed in a single human lifetime. In just under ninety years the tent encampment gave place to the first houses; hotels and halls were built, the place filled with bustling miners, their families, and sundry hangers-on, to flourish while the gold held out. Then it began dwindling, homes and shops being left empty, to crumble eventually and fall down. Two of the hotels still serve beer in a small way. At the Imperial an old lady behind the bar informed me she was eighty-three and had been brought to Ravenswood as a baby when everything was new. She remembered the town of her girlhood as loud with the clatter of trade, and swelling ever louder in the evening when miners gathered in the hotels to sing and seek what amusements were on offer. She told me they were friendly, brawling men. Now, she sits musing behind the bar. In the whole town only half a dozen buildings are still inhabited, standing surrounded by roofless shells, gardens run wild, stairways leading to empty sites, and beyond this a desolate ravaged landscape is being choked by blue flowering Rubber Vine (brought originally, like so many other rampant pests, as an ornamental pot plant). Detritus is everywhere: a tangle of old steel cables and, like some scene from a past war, monumental lumps of broken machinery rusting into the ground, a few loose flaps of iron squeaking in the wind, and the whole place swept by the clear air of human absence.

The cemetery is stark, hot and wind-swept, surrounded by acres of barren, hard-packed ground littered with broken bottles and bits of rusted metal. There I saw a touching sight. The gate squealed; and an elderly women walked in, bringing a basket of flowers. *Flowers*, I thought, in amazement: where in Ravenswood could she get flowers, other than the hated blue Rubber Vine! She was attended by an elderly son carrying two big plastic flasks dripping water. Together, they did the rounds of the gravestones, setting fallen vases upright and filling them, allotting one flower to each grave, and little posies for three in particular, presumably family. They worked for a solid hour, keeping alive the memory of people who had once been the inhabitants of this dying town. They were a repository of the knowledge, without which a whole community would be lost forever.

What a contrast it is to drive down the scarp to the coastal sugar towns. Here fields of tall cane spread their dense green mat over the whole plain. Here the breeze that greets you is heavy with sweet brown smoke and rags of cinders whirling up from the crop which is being burnt clear of undergrowth to be ready for harvesting. Here the people have Italian and Yugoslavian names. Here even so small and remote a town as Innisfail boasts a festival of opera. The Chinese joss-house is one of the only two historic temples of this kind still in operation. It is very noticeable in such a typical Queensland town, being red and gold outside with a brilliant green roof. Inside there is a big drum on a stand, its skin painted with flowers and dragons, and a chunky red bell hung from a frame. Various plants stand round in pots and behind the altar are painted statues of the God of War, the Goddess of Mercy, and Confucius the Teacher. On feast days candles and joss-sticks are lit and gifts of symbolic paper money and tea are offered to the Gods. The temple is still supported by the Chinese community and tended by a handful of old people who live in tiny houses at the back. During the last century, most of the Chinese in this area worked as timber-getters or banana farmers. Then, around 1910, all the land was taken up for sugar planting and big farmers and sugar companies bought them out.

Having a few days to spare before meeting up with my wife for a Barrier Reef holiday, I took the opportunity of driving back inland again and visiting the tobacco-growing districts on the Atherton Tableland.

Motel accommodation in north Queensland can be chancy.

152

At Ravenshoe (not to be confused with Ravenswood) I arrived by nightfall to find, to my relief, the tiny town boasted two motels. I pulled up at the more comfortable looking one and got out, conscious, in a contemptible moment, that my hire-car looked pretty stylish out here, being a new Peugeot – to be confronted with an empty reception office. I rang the bell. No one came. I killed time glancing at some knick-knacks and local craft objects of turned wood in a showcase, then rang again. The manager appeared. But he did not come fully into the room, he stood in the doorway, emanating disapproval. He waited for me to speak first. I asked for a single room. 'Full up, mate,' he said. 'Mate', incidentally can be given an impressive range of meanings. In this perfunctory tone it labelled me as an undesirable outsider; possibly for no more serious offence than the combination called to his mind by my beard, my careless clothes and city accent. 'No worries,' I said, and left. In the carpark area enclosed by the motel units, there were two cars and one truck. At least seventeen of the rooms were unoccupied, and remained so when I drove past early next morning. There was not another town in this wild region for 50 kilometres, I was feeling tired, my fuel tank was almost empty, and the service station was shut. I crossed my fingers that the only remaining accommodation was not also 'full'. This motel had been built at the back of an ugly old bar. I drove into the yard, setting a couple of chained Alsatians barking ferociously and leaping towards my headlamps. Need I say, I got out cautiously, crossed the yard to an OFFICE sign, pointing towards a rather unlikely back door to the bar. I rang the bell provided and out came a plump middle-aged lady of Greek origin. 'A unit?' she repeated my request in a voice accustomed to being heard over the hubbub of heavy drinkers in that timber-getting community, 'you can take your pick, love, I've got twelve still vacant. It isn't the height of the season,' she joked and roared with laughter. An older person, who was her mother perhaps, standing at a nearby kitchen window, looked out at us and laughed in sympathy. Cheerful, welcoming laughter. I could have hugged them both. 'Don't mind the dogs,' she said as she unlocked my room for me, 'they'll only chew your leg off if I give them the word. OK?' The following morning, when I was woken at dawn as I had requested, the same Greek lady served me with a massive breakfast. I asked her if she ever took time off from the job. 'What for?' she asked in genuine surprise, 'it's my life, this hotel. I love it here.'

Farther north lies Cape Tribulation (what a tough time Captain Cook had back in 1770). Here you can visit the splendid Daintree Rainforest – provided the conservationists manage to hold out and exert enough moral pressure on the Commonwealth government to prevent the Queensland state government, with its worship of so-called 'free market forces', from smashing the whole lot down for the sake of quick profits. The rainforest is an unforgettable experience: silence enhances the occasional bird-call, sudden warm rain clicks against the dense foliage far overhead, where leaves hang bright with silver light, and every gust of wind shakes down jewels of raindrops long after the clouds have passed, and the sun shines beyond the permanent airy shade of the forest. For any but experienced bushwalkers, it is definitely advisable to stick to the paths provided. Not only can you get lost easily, but the undergrowth is thick with thorny vines and stinging trees. A less energetic way to view the forest is to take a Daintree River cruise and glide between banks fringed with tropical mangroves.

This area runs up the east coast of Cape York, that tapering finger of land ending in the northmost point of Australia.

I have never been across to the western side of the peninsula, to the shores of the Gulf of Carpentaria, but I believe

154

Normanton is a place not to be missed. There are almost no metalled roads or bridges in the area, so it is a matter of choosing the time for such a trip with care, or taking the train – the famous rattletrap Gulflander Rail Motor. The old colonial buildings with their wide verandas and rusting iron roofs seem to have survived there with very little modification. In places like this, the important visual element is not cohesiveness but isolation. Each building tends to stand by itself in a broad space of flat ground; so, between the buildings, the horizon may still be seen. The humour of a community battling to survive is evident in occasional foibles of design, or bars called the Grand. The landscape beyond is dotted with galvanised metal windmills (for pumping water) and iron water tanks set high on spindly steel frames. At this point I must digress briefly to say something about Queensland domestic architecture.

The key to it all is corrugated iron, which is often and most unfairly dismissed as an inferior roofing material. It is, on the contrary, very efficient and, being so light, the roof does not need the clumsy structure of trusses and slats required to support tiles. It is also highly portable and simple to erect – both of which were useful properties to builders in remote areas. The combination of three features created the characteristic Queensland house: verandahs, a foundation of wooden stumps, and the iron roof. The result is a style at once distinctive, aesthetically delightful and comfortable to live in. Where the climate is more temperate, families tend to live quite a lot of the time on their verandah, sitting there in the evening, eating there, and even sleeping there for coolness. In the tropics, they are more likely to live in the dim cool interior of the house, using the verandahs as a shady means of buffering the fierce heat outside. Mosquito nets at night are necessary in many places if you are to get a decent night's sleep. But a debased preference for the pseudo-

155

respectability of brick has been made practical in these hot places by the availability of home air-conditioning units. So, with new houses, one no longer looks in through the charming recesses of shady verandahs to a house left permanently open for the breeze, but at the blank, shut façade of brick with flush windows (one of which will house the projecting back-end of a cooler unit) and drawn curtains. Though hardly any new houses are being made to the traditional pattern, there are, fortunately, many thousands of old ones still in use right down to Brisbane and beyond.

The roads in these areas are extremely rough and unpredictable. Useful maps are available from the RACQ, who should also be consulted at all stages about local conditions. Between most centres flights are available by light aircraft. And, of course, you should not overlook the pleasures of travelling by boat where possible.

A very glamorous-sounding holiday is to cruise up the Whitsunday Passage aboard the *Golden Plover*, a two-masted sailing ship which looks so convincingly straight out of the nineteenth century that it's been used in several films. By all accounts, though, the trip tends rather towards boy scout and girl guide jollity, with joke sessions around the camp fire at each evening's landfall. But under the down-market homeliness, the passenger is, apparently well cared for, and offered quite a lot of extra activities, such as snorkelling, diving and learning to wind surf. There is also the paradisal element to be taken into account – the blue, blue waters, the heat of a tropical sun, palm trees nodding along the shore, and a mountainous coast thickly covered with rainforest. Quite the stuff of dreams. And the cost for seven days and nights is not exorbitant once you have got yourself to Proserpine where the ship departs from.

This could be the ultimate 'away from it all' holiday, lounging on deck while the sails thump and the rigging creaks, gliding slowly past the lush islands of the Passage, which is formed by the Great Barrier Reef.

The reef, Australia's principal tourist attraction, is over 1200 kilometres long, stretching right up to the coast of New Guinea. Narrow in the north – in some places a mere 12 kilometres wide – the coral formation is immensely wide in the south – off Townsville it extends some 300 kilometres out to sea. Typical of such formations, the reef is studded with islands (over 700 of them) from which the explorer may set off to view the coral. Living coral is found underwater, so the holiday-maker spends many hours swimming around wearing a snorkel and goggles, or drifting in a glass-bottomed boat to marvel at the formations below.

My wife and I went to stay on Dunk Island. This was the first time we had been up that way, despite having lived in Queensland for twenty-five years. We flew from Townsville out across the channel to the resort. The blaze of colour seen from an aircraft is hard to describe. Shallow water lies like a vast mottled opal, glowing with incredible variations of green and blue. Out past the wild romantic shores of Hinchinbrook Island which rises, entirely cloaked in rainforest, to the splendid peak of Mount Bowen (1143 metres, or 3650 feet). Captain Cook named the island after the family seat of his patron, George Montagu Dunk, First Lord of the Admiralty. Then, when he reached it the following day, he named Dunk Island itself.

As we got out of the plane, the whole party of a dozen or so passengers laden with expectations of blazing sunshine, white beaches and days spent sprawled under palm trees, we had to run for cover from a sudden downpour of rain. Never mind, we assured each other, laughing optimistically, typical of showers in these latitudes, this will be gone in ten minutes. Half an hour later, the rain did stop and we sauntered to the resort while the welcoming staff looked after our baggage.

But the clouds had come to stay. For five days of the week we had booked – and the cost is high – the sky remained obstinately overcast.

Dunk Island lies inshore of the main reef, which is a three-hour trip out to sea. The sea had turned too rough for any boats to make the trip. Each day we reserved our seats, only to be disappointed. Meanwhile, we were, in fact, having a wonderful holiday. The food and service left little to be desired. Since everything, except drinks and tickets out to the reef, are included in the all-up price, we helped ourselves to tennis rackets, golf clubs, or bows and arrows, and trooped off to these various amusements; or, more often, simply walked round the island which is small, mountainous, densely forested and wonderfully peaceful. The place was alive with birds and butterflies. Apart from the mindless music, blaring each night in the main entertainment building with its bar and dancefloor, the peace was a great restorative. Then, on our sixth day there, out came the sun, the sea grew calm, the boat departed for the reef. And for two days we swam, sunbaked, sailed catamarans, marvelled at coral formations, and returned home swearing that this was the most perfect place imaginable for a holiday.

I suppose the main surprise of a resort like Dunk is having to *go* out to the reef in the first place: I expected to simply wade there from the hotel chalet. The next surprise was that there is nothing to be seen on the surface. The boat anchors in shallow water near a tiny hummock of white pulverised shells and dead coral euphemistically called an island. And that's that. I thought we would be confronted by the reef stretching as far as the eye could see, north and south, branches of coral obligingly stuck up above the surface. No. Nothing but flat water. Then we were issued with snorkelling gear and ferried to the little island in a glass-bottomed boat. We looked down from the disappointing world we had reached into a miraculous paradise of strange forms: branched coral with bright blue tips, fans of frail orange twigs and white brain shapes, giant clams opened to show mushroom-like ruffles of the richest purple and dark green, while myriads of fish, bright as jewels, fed around the reef. Perhaps in common with most good things of life, the reef is not at all what you expect it to be. And one needs a little while to adjust, in order to appreciate what is actually there. Perhaps this description I have given also evokes false images, despite the fact that I have tried to represent the place as fairly as possible. But let me assure anyone who is tempted to go there that I have never yet met a single person who regretted going. The main thing to bear in mind is the volatility of the weather. This is the tropics, after all. And the one thing the resort promotion compaigns omit to point out is that a tremendous amount of rain falls up there. Of course, for visitors like my wife, who does not enjoy great heat, the rain can be a blessing in any case.

Returning home from Dunk Island, when I thought back on the experience, the curious fact is that, apart from the pleasures of bush-walking around the mountain in light rain, my memories were almost exactly those I criticised the tourist brochures for so exclusively promising: palm trees, the white beaches where we bathed, brilliant blue water, a giant turtle which swam just under the surface alongside our catamaran on the last morning, a seafood banquet, and the friendly, efficient service. These things are, after all, there. The point, I suppose, is that you have to give it time to grow on you, rather than expecting to be hit over the head at every turn with the experience of a tropical paradise.

There are certain clichés about life in Australia which have become clichés precisely because they are true and yet defy description. Among these are the fear of bushfires, which I mentioned in the chapter on Victoria, and the fear of floods.

159

Floods are particularly extreme in the north. Our river systems are characteristically serpentine because so much of the land is flat. The water flows slowly, lazily, wandering through the scrub and towns. The Brisbane River, for example, becomes so convoluted as it nears the sea, its horse-shoe bends so exaggerated, that it nearly doubles back on itself to form islands where the city and inner suburbs line its banks. When it floods and the overflow comes raging down from the headwaters, the volume cannot be discharged fast enough. Even a river as large as this one may rise above its normal level an almost unbelievable amount. The record flood, in 1893, when 70 inches (almost 2 metres) of rain fell during two storms before further registration was impossible on the instruments available, the low-lying parts of south Brisbane were entirely submerged. During the 1955 floods in New South Wales, the Hunter River at Singleton and the Macquarie River at Wellington both rose by more than 50 feet (15 metres). Looking through the record of floods, except for certain dry patches (such as the period 1922–30) there is usually a flood somewhere or other in the country – and, as often as not, other regions can be enduring a drought at the same time.

If the rare flood rains strike in the semi-desert areas of the outback, the outcome can be spectacular indeed. In 1949 when Cooper's Creek flowed, where the gradient is only 17 centimetres per kilometre, the normally dry creek became a river 13 kilometres wide.

It is no accident that I have put Queensland last of the states and delayed writing about Brisbane in particular till now. How can one write of one's hometown (even, as in my case, an adoptive hometown) with even a modicum of objectivity? I see it with despair, with love, with contempt and exultancy. I avoid it. I am drawn to it. I despise the civic vandalism that has erased almost all evidence of our memories

160

with the demolition of entire blocks of city buildings, and I despise the vulgarity of the city that has been rushed up to replace our old one – in exactly the same measure as my heart leaps at some surviving reminder of the way things were. This was once, until the mid-1950s, the biggest and most hygienic shantytown in the world; the main streets flanked by iron awnings held up on spindly pavement-posts. Outrageously unconcerned with appearances or notions of metropolitan respectability, Brisbane was warm, eccentric, a little bit wild, also a bit sleepy, and altogether lovable.

As I remember it, problems were characteristically met with a common expression, 'She'll be right, mate!' – a comfortable, capable unflappability, laid-back and perhaps lazy. *She* is a colloquial usage, here, in place of *it* or *everything*. A rough equivalent might be: 'Don't you worry about that!'

Although not born there, I went to school in Brisbane and that's where I lived during the vital teenage years. The city as I once knew it has been razed to the ground. In its place we are presented with air-conditioned, sanitised comfort about as endearing as a hospital ward. The agglomeration of human errors and foibles which once made up the sum of architectural interest, bar a couple of truly handsome public buildings islanded in the cheerful hugger-mugger of low-grade fancifulness, have now been replaced by bland bad taste in steel and glass, plus an overdose of self-congratulatory propaganda.

The problem is that the city burgesses have shown themselves as not only without a sense of style but without a sense of humour either. King George Square in the centre of town was a unique catastrophe of follies, the centrepiece being an imposing city hall which contrived to have the best of all worlds, with neo-classical Bank of England columns right along the front, a dome (albeit a shallow one) and a Greek pediment. Still not satisfied, the ambitious architect wanted a tower, to be, if possible, a lightweight version of St Mark's campanile in Venice – which he balanced on top of the whole building between the pediment and the dome. Some genius thought to plant palm trees outside, right along the front. And splendid specimens they grew to be. The final touch was a broad granite stairway leading up to the portico. King George Square, being on a slope, there were more steps on the right-hand end than on the left, so the stairway presented the eye with a triangle tipping the entire concoction off balance. The banana-republic palm trees rustled and flourished splendidly. There was also a statue of King Goerge V in the square, which had its own history of miscalculations. The tall sandstone plinth had been built, flanked by a couple of bronze lions when, so it is said, the council took fright at the cost of the equestrian statue being cast for them and altered the commission. They would make do with a three-quarter size version in the interests of economy. In due course, the statue arrived. And it was not at all bad. But, inspired as ever, they set it up back-to-front, with the horse's tail presented to the city and a somewhat irritable monarch appearing to ride straight for the city hall doors, his dignity not enhanced by finding his lions mounted above subterranean public toilets and the roadway between him and those asymmetrical granite steps cluttered by a taxi rank. A nice old art-nouveau cinema, the Tivoli, stood opposite to complete the picture.

Well, the burgesses eventually saw this folly for what it was, but failed to see the charm of it. Down came the lot, the Tivoli, the statue, the lions, the toilets, the granite stairway and the palm trees. Apparently convinced that a square must have some *use*, they gouged out a huge underground parking station, the flat roof of which became the new square, ruthlessly level and regular. King George, deposed from his lofty plinth, was later put in his place on a substitute made of concrete blocks and turned to face the right way. His lions were taken off him and awarded to the burgesses themselves as suitable ornaments to flank the entrance to the building. Now that the level of the square had been raised and the wonderful balancing act removed, the triangular stairs were no longer required. The palm trees, which had been uprooted and miraculously kept alive, were replanted, but too close to the building for comfort – and there they stand today as witnesses to the deed, crowded up against the wall, over-shadowed by that sad travesty of Venice-cum-Greece-cum-Bank of England.

Nevertheless, and losses aside, Brisbane has much to offer. Not least, its magnificent climate. If you like hot weather which is still not the furnace of a full equatorial summer, Brisbane might be just the place for you. This is a balmy, damp heat, scarcely waning more than a couple of degrees at night. The summers are apt to burst into late-afternoon thunderstorms, excessively loud and lusciously wet as only tropical rain ever is, water swirling across streets and cas-cading down gutters, then switching off just as suddenly as it began, to make way for a blinding rush of sunshine that sweeps curlicues of steam along the bitumen. As for winter, this is, by anyone's standard, simply perfect. The weather stays dependably sunny, with swimming temperatures all year round and crisp nights.

The problem for the tourist lies in what to do and what to see. This is a place for living in rather than visiting. Perhaps the most memorable day will not be the one spent in the spacious art gallery with its sketchy collection, or sightseeing from the top of a nearby hill aggrandised with the name Mount Coot-tha, but chugging up river to the Lone Pine Sanctuary, a small wildlife park specialising in koala bears. Here you may hold them and be photographed with a placid heavy specimen clutched in your arms. Here you

163

may get a good close look at emus and touch a kangaroo. Incidentally, the river journey itself is a pleasant meander between wooded banks occasionally cleared for riverside suburbs.

The nearby Gold Coast offers a kind of Las Vegas on the sea. And when I say 'on the sea', I mean so close as to be almost in it. The slender apartment towers stand right by the sand. Looking along the beach at Surfers' Paradise, the clean lines of this futuristic city are reflected in wet sand as each wave sweeps back from the shore, leaving a multitude of surf-riders to pick themselves up and charge back out into the swell to ride another roller. Surfers' Paradise makes no pretence of being other than hedonistic. Beauty parlours, health studios, restaurants, discos and fashion shops fill the lives and empty the pockets of holiday-makers who come all year round at a rate of over 3 million annually.

There are still several very beautiful beaches in the area, notably Burleigh Heads and Currumbin. Currumbin also boasts a private bird sanctuary where visitors go to feed flocks of wild parrots. The brilliantly coloured birds are as fearless as Trafalgar Square pigeons and perch on your head and shoulders in the expectation of being fed.

Just inland of the 34-kilometre strip of the Gold Coast's over-developed real-estate, Lamington Plateau rises on the horizon. For bushwalkers, there is nowhere better in the whole country. This rainforested plateau offers everything from graded walks with signposts to wonderful wilderness areas where you need a compass, food for several days, and someone in the party with experience of surviving in the bush. When I was a member of the Brisbane Bushwalkers' Club in the 1950s and 1960s, this was one of our favourite areas. I've hacked my way through vicious vines and ducked to avoid the dreadful stinging leaves of the Gympie Tree, dangled off sheer cliffs and sweated out the long slog to the

164

peaks, slushed knee-deep in liquid mud and been lost and exhausted in dense forest ... and come out of it each time with a deeper love of the place, counting the days till I could be back there again. One of the great away-from-it-all holidays is to stay in the cabin accommodation at Binna Burra. The comforts are spartan, but the welcome in the communal dining hall is wonderful.

The Gold Coast lies an hour's coach journey south of Brisbane. Roughly the same distance north is the Sunshine Coast, stretching from Caloundra to Noosa. In my view, these beaches are more various and beautiful than the Gold Coast and the development not so hectic. Busy tourist places, nonetheless, they tend to attract families. Caloundra is especially fine for young children, offering calm backwaters as well as the open surf.

Between the Gold Coast and the Sunshine Coast lie three islands sheltering the mouth of Moreton Bay where the Brisbane River flows into the sea: Stradbroke, Moreton and Bribie. Each is between 30–40 kilometres long. On the seaward side they have glorious open beaches and on the landward side sheltered shorelines fronting on to the bay. Once, when I was swimming in the waters on this enormous, shallow bay, some friends on shore at Stradbroke began waving at me and jumping up and down, pointing. I waved back. A few moments later a huge shape, like a dark cloud passing just under the water's surface, floated gently between me and them. Only as it was going, did I realise this was a giant manta ray, probably twelve or fourteen feet across, the tip of its 'wing' wavering sensitively and gracefully in the current within arm's reach. It was small comfort to be assured, when I got back to safety, that the creature was harmless.

Just as the Gold Coast has a magnificent hinterland, so has the Sunshine Coast. Over 200 years ago, in May 1770,

Captain Cook sighted a spectacular cluster of peaks on the east coast. He wrote in his Journal, 'They are remarkable on account of their singular elevation which . . . resembles Glass Houses, which occasioned my giving them that name.' The variety of the Glasshouse Mountains offers a range of pleasures to the visitor: you can choose between a leisurely climb taking no more than a quarter of an hour, or an arduous attempt with grappling-irons and ropes to master sheer cliffs, or the less spectacular but still tiring climb to the top of the largest of the group, Mount Beerwah, or – like most people – remain simply content with looking at them from a distance. At the foot of this mountain cluster – it can hardly be called a range, since each peak rises separately from the plain – the pineapple farms are an added attraction.

To the north of the Glasshouse Mountains rises the escarpment to the Blackall Ranges. From the top of this scarp, near the little towns of Montville and Maleny, a spectacular panorama spreads out at your feet. This is probably the best vantage point along the eastern seaboard for getting a clear idea of the agricultural districts of the coastal plain and of the fertile plateau to the west. Local crops are bananas, pineapples, guava, avocados, ginger, citrus fruits and sugar-cane.

The best known of a number of traditional Tibetan ashrams is also to be found in this district. Individuals and families live permanently on the ashram with their Tibetan teachers, but, as with others of its kind, visitors may arrange with the monks to stay for a meditative retreat. Detailed information about such ashrams is available from the Buddhist Centre in north Sydney.

One of my friends at boarding-school came from Nambour, which is the nearest town to the ashram. If I had been told then, in 1950, that close to his father's farm we would one day see saffron-robed monks in residence and that

166

their followers would be ordinary suburban Australians, I'm sure I would have dismissed the idea as crazy. Now, I take it as one more measure of how far we have come. Not only are Catholics and Protestants on such casual, amicable terms that they have ceased to be wary or hostile about one another's faith, but there are practising Buddhists, Jews, and Muslims, adherents of all manner of religions, and we are able to give them room to worship as they please without the least friction.

The secular side of the story is even more startling. One finds whole suburbs of our main cities where English is hardly spoken, and we have yet to experience racial tension there. Perhaps we'd do well to keep our fingers crossed; but personally I think that integration is being achieved and will continue to be peaceful. Melbourne has the third-largest Greek population of any city anywhere, including Greece. Cabramatta in Sydney is a little Vietnam, with some eighty Vietnamese restaurants and scarcely a single letter of English on the display signs in shop windows.

Of course, the old Aussie character still exists. Perhaps nowhere more than in Queensland, which has felt the impact of refugees and of the immigration scheme far less than any other part of the country.

In the July 1987 edition of the *Law Institute Journal* (vol. 61, no. 6) I came upon the following item, which is almost too good to be true. The editor himself apparently thought the same, because it appeared in the 'Hearsay' column. The story, about a Queensland farmer suing for damages after his horse was hit by a car, embodies the quintessential slowness of bush humour.

Defence counsel: After the accident, didn't someone come over to you and ask how you felt?
Farmer: Yes, I believe that is so.

Defence counsel: And didn't you tell him that you never felt better in your life?

Farmer: Yes, I guess I did.

(*Defence counsel sits down. Plaintiff's counsel stands up.*)

Plaintiff's counsel: Will you tell His Honour the circumstances in which you made the response?

Farmer: Yes. Not long after the accident, my horse, which had sustained broken legs, was thrashing around. A policeman ... came up to the horse, put his revolver to its ear and shot it dead. He then went over to my dog, which had a broken back and was howling miserably. He put his revolver to the dog's ear and shot it. Then he came to me and asked: 'How do you feel?'

9   *Cool Hothouse*

CANBERRA

When the Australian states formed a federation in 1901, discussions concerning a possible capital city had been going on for thirty years. The idea was to choose a site which would be sufficiently far from each of the two main rivals, Sydney and Melbourne, to remain neutral. The most favoured site was at Eden, where there is a magnificent harbour, Twofold Bay, but this was rejected on the grounds that the harbour might be *too* good, and might develop into a port to outstrip both the contesting cities.

So, as second-best, a site was chosen up on the Monaro plateau, set in a saucer of hills, beside the tiny Molonglo River. This is a beautiful location, though the administrative city which has grown there does have that somewhat sanitised unreality common to artificially created capital cities the world over.

The streets are designed as interlocking circles developed from a basic triangular grid. The result can be pure confusion. The first time I drove there, my nose alternately glued to the windscreen and the map, repeatedly ending up in some cul-de-sac or recognising with a sinking heart the same apartment block and the same shopping centre I passed a few minutes earlier, I began cursing the place as a navigator's nightmare.

Once you know your way round, Canberra is a breeze, the easiest city in the world for driving (and everyone does drive). You wonder how you ever found it confusing. During the so-called rush-hour, traffic moves out along arterial roads at a steady 80 km/h – to the envy of Sydneysiders and Melbournians. But, if you are a stranger, not knowing the routes

169

and having to find an address, give yourself plenty of time
... and try to see the funny side, to prevent being reduced
to a snarling, vicious wreck. On that first occasion, when I
finally arrived at my friend's house, he brushed my com-
plaints aside: 'It's easy,' he said, 'all you need to remember
is that if you wish to reach somewhere over to your right,
turn left. And if you wish to reach somewhere over to your
left, turn right!'

Later, when we came to live in this comfortable city with
its wonderfully clear air and superb public services, we
encountered another theory about the road system. 'The
truth is this,' our informant explained. 'With devilish
cunning, the planners amused themselves by setting the place
up as a psychological trap. The idea was to undermine the
institution of marriage. How? Well, to drive from any point
A to any point B, their scheme allows you at least two
possible routes, each circuitous and each of identical length.
Inevitably, wife and husband disagree about which to take.
She prefers this one, he prefers that. Since neither can be
proved quicker than the other, the argument remains
unsolved and the parting of the ways has, literally, begun.'
He roared with delighted laughter at this accusation against
his chosen city and regaled us with outrageous tales of
bureaucratic plots to baffle the public. I was entertained, of
course. But, knowing something of Canberra's background,
I sensed a slightly hysterical edge to the humour, nonetheless.

An international competition was held in 1911 for a city
plan. This was the beginning for Canberra: till then, only a
few buildings and a tiny hamlet occupied the site.

All things considered – including the miserly prize
money – the winning design was surprisingly good. It came
from an American, a follower of Frank Lloyd Wright, named
Walter Burley Griffin. But no sooner had our Federal
Government (temporarily housed in Melbourne) approved

170

it, than they got cold feet and appointed a board to examine it and report back to parliament. Apparently misconstruing the whole point of Burley Griffin's design, they put up a rival plan of their own and promptly began building it. The resultant mess was saved in 1958 only with the establishment of the National Capital Development Commission. Too late to salvage more than a skeleton of the original road scheme and the situation of a few key buildings, they did at least create a fine artificial lake (the original plan had called for three) and something of the ceremonial vistas. Now, thirty years down the track, the whole concept has had to be re-thought, because Canberra is not just an administrative centre. Nor has its population stopped at the projected 25,000. A quarter of a million people live there now, and it has developed satellite shopping towns at Belconnen in the north and Woden in the south. One commonly meets young adults who were born there and know no other home. Canberra is becoming a living city. This is a most fascinating process to watch. It has occurred dramatically, in my own observation, since I first went there on a visit. The layout is less monumental, certainly less coordinated and beautiful than the original design, but also more human.

Among other distinctions, such as housing all the foreign embassies, the national war memorial, and the Defence Force Academy, Canberra is also where the Governor-General has his residence. The role of the Governor-General is, in the opinion of many Australians, anachronistic not to say anomalous. Is he Head of State or isn't he? Well, that depends.

The colonial Governors were appointed by Westminster and were representatives of the British Government. This was a clear function which lasted well beyond the granting of self-determination, even beyond Federation in 1901 when Australia became, at least nominally, an independent nation. It lasted until the Balfour Report of 1926. In 1926, the

Governor-General's role was defined as being the same in relation to the Commonwealth Parliament as was the monarch's, thereby making him the King's (or, later, Queen's) representative (whereas each State Governor – another anomalous situation – remains technically as a representative of the British Government).

The full Gilbertian humour of the situation did not emerge until 1975 when a Governor-General, who later that year precipitated the greatest political crisis in our history, visited Nepal for the coronation of King Birenda. The Nepalese officials went into a huddle with the Australian High Commissioner in India to sort out the protocol. What precisely, they asked, was this Governor-General? Was he the Head of State, and thus due for Head of State pecking-order during the ceremony? In which case, how did it happen that Queen Elizabeth II also listed among her titles, Queen of Australia?

The fact was that the Queen was (and still is) Australian Head of State, and the Governor-General represented her when she was not on Australian territory. What role he could assume at an official function *abroad* became a curly question, involving the selection of which suite of rooms he should occupy, where he should be seated at table, behind whom and before whom should he walk in the procession, and what the band should play as a salute. It resulted in a full-scale diplomatic conference which tested the subtlety and ingenuity of the foreign services of both nations.

The only time I was ever invited to the Governor-General's residence, Yarralumla House, I found the occasion dismally stiff and ponderous. This was a musical soirée with an audience of guests drawn largely from artists in various fields. I knew most of the performers and many of the audience; but all trace of spontaneity was squeezed out of them by their too-formal clothes, the suffocating observance of seniority, the room's woolly acoustics, and the ersatz conversation of people so carefully watching what they said that they in fact said nothing. I was pleased to have attended, simply for the novelty, but I was even more pleased to get away and breathe a good fill of Canberra's fresh evening air.

The scale of our parliamentary comedy may only be appreciated when one considers that we have eight separate State or Territory Governments, all but three of which are replete with upper as well as lower houses, in addition to a Federal Parliament. So, there are six Governors (representatives of the Parliament at Westminster), a Governor-General (representative of the monarch), and fifteen chambers of elected representatives ... all to govern 16 million people, a population that is equivalent to that of compressed New York city. Every year there is an election in some part of Australia, often two or three. And voting is compulsory.

I, personally, look forward to the day when we declare a republic, cut the ties, and assume total responsibility for ourselves. Hopefully, when that happens, this ridiculous clutter with its petty divisions of power, will be swept away. It is not a question of repudiating the past, far from it; it is a question of accepting the past as being the past, and moving forward to welcome the future.

Canberra is surrounded by its own territory, the Australian Capital Territory, which extends roughly 100 kilometres north/south and 40 kilometres east/west. The southern extremity reaches almost to the verges of the snow country. And, indeed, winter sports are a great feature of life for Canberrans. So, despite the fact that the alpine resorts are actually in New South Wales and Victoria, I have placed them in this chapter. For the visitor, also, they are most easily and conveniently reached from Canberra.

I must admit that I am further persuaded in this by the amusement it affords me to conclude a book about Australia –

so famous as a land of sunshine and surf beaches – in the snowfields.

I am not a skier, so I have had to rely on other people's information to offer this summary. My own visits to the Australian Alps have always been in spring to see the great carpet of wildflowers, or in summer for long walks over the bare slopes and ridges, when the snow has long since melted. Not only do I not ski, but I have a horror of cold weather. Any reader who enjoys the snow and winter sports can safely add a heavy dose of enthusiasm to the next few pages.

The snowfields, considered as a whole (and taking no account of the state border cutting them in half by an imaginary line), boast about a dozen resorts. Much the same conditions apply, whether the resorts are in New South Wales or Victoria.

The area is greater than that of the snowfields in Switzerland – even though the mountains are nowhere near so spectacular. Some resorts have full residential facilities, others provide only chairlifts and restaurant services. Before contemplating a trip to this area in the season, it is advisable to contact information offices such as the New South Wales tourist office in Sydney, or Ski Victoria in Melbourne. Only by making a detailed comparison of the resorts, their cost, special features and attractions will you be in a position to choose where to go. Some, such as Guthega and Mount Selwyn are especially attractive to beginners and family groups. Others may appeal to a more expert clientele. The season, incidentally, lasts for only ten to twelve weeks, beginning in June.

A great deal of excitement centres on the newly built Skitube which takes skiers by train through a tunnel in the mountain to a new resort known as Mount Blue Cow. From Bullock's Flat near Jindabyne the railway operates 24 hours a day, with an underground stop at Perisher Valley on the

174

way. The journey to Mount Blue Cow takes only quarter of an hour but brings you to an area previously remote and difficult to reach. A whole bonanza of technological wizardry is there for those who warm to that kind of thing. You needn't even risk the chance of being disappointed by the snow when you get there, because at the Skitube terminal a huge video continuously screens live pictures from the summit of the mountain to show what conditions are like. Even using Skitube as a non-skiing sightseer, the effect, I must say, is magical: emerging into an almost untouched valley where there is no road access at all.

Facilities at Mount Blue Cow include a 750-seat bistro and various other eating and drinking places, but no overnight accommodation. Thredbo, by contrast, is set up on the model of a Swiss alpine village. Indeed, when you stand among this cluster of chalets and mountain lodges, the rest of Australia seems half a world away. Thredbo has 100 kilometres of ski trails, suitable for sporting people at all levels. There are four chairlifts and six T-bars, plus multi-million-dollar equipment which can manufacture 35,000 cubic metres of fresh snow a week if nature is disobliging enough to withold sufficient free supplies. You can't be disappointed. Nothing is left to chance these days. The nearby Perisher Valley/Smiggin Holes resort similarly covers all needs. During the season they employ more than a hundred resident professional ski instructors. Even larger than these is the Mount Buller resort in Victoria, where the ski-lifts boast a capacity for handling 26,131 persons per hour.

All I have to say is that, having felt those biting black winds come sweeping around bare mountain slopes even in summer, the very thought of winter up there is enough to send me running for the beach.

But devotees regard me as a philistine in this respect. Even at the end of a day, the mountain resorts offer a scene which they find irresistibly enticing: the bright restaurant a hubbub of competitive skiing yarns, log fires blazing cosily, the entire clientele united in sociability by having this consuming interest in snow in common. Meanwhile, outside, latecomers trudge over the yard, flushed and triumphant. A bitter wind blows down from the upper slopes. A few promising flakes are driven to hurtle soundlessly against the glass. The warmth is a positive expression of wellbeing.

Australia's highest mountain, Mount Kosciusko, was named after a Polish count who explored the area in the late 1830s. He returned to Sydney with news which, from the point of view of a young colony, was even more gripping than snow-covered mountains – gold. The governor at the time, George Gipps, being a farsighted man, asked for the count's word of honour that he would not mention this discovery to anyone, because the consequences to the stability of a society only just liberated from the convict system was too dreadful to contemplate. How right he was. Gold, when news of it could no longer be suppressed, set its mark on the Australian ethos every bit as vividly as the convict system already had.

It is at Mount Kosciusko that I end this journey through Australia. I was there last March, at the least-favoured time of year, autumn. Autumn, without the advantages of winter snow, spring flowers or summer mildness, is a time when sudden changes of temperature sweep in across the mountains, when racing clouds seem to materialise from nowhere (because, to an Australian, a horizon among mountains is so much closer than the horizon seen from across the plains), dramatically heralding treacherous cold gales, or, dispersing just as precipitately, leaving the sun to blaze from a blindingly blue sky on a landscape where, being above the winter snow-line, no trees survive to offer shade.

My wife and I, with our photographer friends Wesley

Stacey and Narelle Perroux, stood looking out over the bare flank of the range with its icy little streams knocking rocks together, and delicious crystalline water swirling invitingly around boulders. High on the ridges, great swathes and saddles of snow still held the coldness of last winter. The tail-end of a wind that had made us shiver went scurrying among spiky heath and low-grown bushes and was gone. Remorseless sunshine came gliding over us, bringing a million flies. The saddles of residual snow shone dazzlingly white, as if one were looking through a hole in the blue-green mountainside at sunlit clouds beyond. And my thoughts lingered on this unique continent, ringed by three oceans, and on the extraordinary diversity of the huge land, which lay below me while I stood on its highest point ...

EPILOGUE

I cannot do it: I thought I could, but I can't. I thought it would be entertaining to end up in the snow, preferably evoking a blizzard in which a party of ill-equipped tourists might be stranded ... But there is a truer ending and one which the shape of the book demands: my own return home – not to Brisbane, nor yet to England, but to Barragga Bay, where I live and intend to remain living for as many years ahead as I can foresee.

I will indulge in one last flutter with blizzardly weather by beginning this homecoming a couple of months ago, at a time when the Snowy Mountains had their heaviest falls for quarter of a century. Even in Bombala, a tiny town on the edge of the plateau, well below the foothills of the mountains, the snowdrifts were more than a metre deep. The town was cut off and the electricity lines were down, leaving people without power or supplies. As I came through from Canberra, heading east towards the coast, I had to pass the turn-off to Bombala. There I saw warning signs set up at the roadside and the blue flashing lights of police cars parked by the junction. I drove on along the highway (the mountains dwindling in my rear-vision mirror) till conditions changed and I found I was gradually emerging from the snowy weather of that grim morning – only to plunge into thick fog. Then the clouds must have begun to break, high above, because I found myself enveloped in luminosity. At times the fog grew so brilliant it was like being right inside the source of light itself. As I approached the lip of the escarpment, the fog began to disperse, till I was driving through patches of clear

178

morning sunlight where the snow had already melted and the greenness of the paddocks was restored – only to plunge back into another wintery patch, the smudged white landscape punctuated by black sticks and shrubs, not a single bird to be seen, just a few sheep moving slowly under their weight of ice-laden wool. And again into that bright otherworld, with parrots and the astoundingly colourful rainbow lorikeets perched like huge active flowers in the tree tops, fossicking for the first pickings of spring.

On the mountain road winding down to the coastal plain, I seemed to have come to another country altogether. I pulled up and got out of my car. The weather was brisk but pleasant. I marvelled at the contrast, considering that those snowbound areas were a mere half hour's drive back there. I rang my wife to tell her I was safely down, despite the condition of the road, and that I would be home in a little over an hour's time.

Throughout the Bega Valley dairy farming area the pastures looked succulent, creeks and dams full of water. Cattle grazed, contented and plump. Once again, I stopped the car to savour the change like a miraculous deliverance. One lazy crow flew across the road in front of me, calling a couple of times in a bored tone, a hawk hung in the still, blue air. Surrounded by hills and valleys of productive land, the sun positively warm, I thought of the citizens of Bombala holed up in their isolated township without power. I wondered why they didn't all pack their belongings and move down here. But, of course, this presumes people never want trouble or discomfort in their lives, whereas trouble is not separable from life. And trouble may take far more malignant forms than a community united by temporary privation and isolation – which gave me pause to think again about the phenomenon of the immigrant: the long sea journey, the willingness to face uncertainty and even danger.

Epilogue

Reaching the coast, I drove through gentle, forested scenery, coming upon the occasional lake, where black swans floated sedately and pelicans stood at the margins preening their breasts with those unlikely beaks. And, looking seaward from the bridge across the mouth of each lake, I saw the surf pound against a sandbar in the eternal cycle of closing and reopening the way to these wetlands.

As soon as I arrived home, I peeled off layers of woollen clothing and went for a swim (though I confess I ran out much faster than I went in), just to confirm the extremity of the contrast with those freezing conditions up on the range, where police vehicles doubtless still stood parked at the Bombala turn-off, blue strobe lights flashing. My wife and I ate a late lunch out on the verandah. We lounged in summer clothes, looking down at the water of our little bay with its lovely curved sandy beach, no other house in sight, and watched waves sparkle against the cliffs of the opposite headland. A pair of sea-eagles elevated majestically from the trees in the spotted-gum forest up to our left and drifted high above.

At this remote house, we do not have electricity; our refrigerator runs on bottle gas. At night we use candles and oil lamps. Our water supply is rainwater collected from the roof in two large tanks. I joked that some of the snow from Bombala would be useful to top up our supplies. My wife replied that we might console ourselves because, whatever happened, our electricity could not be cut off by anything.

A small fishing trawler from the nearby town of Bermagui came chugging in past the headland, which is an unusual event, so a school of fish must be running close inshore. We sat watching for dolphins while we ate the rest of our pâté and sipped cool drinks, knowing that dolphins are usually around when there is feed for them. We think of them as old friends.

180

Within a few days of this, we expected a visit from a young Chinese writer, Sang Ye, whose book of interviews, *Chinese Profiles*, had made a considerable impact in Beijing. He would probably stay only a night or two, but enough to give us plenty of time for talking. One of the beauties of living here (and we settled fourteen years ago) is that our friends and visitors generally stay, so we see more of them, though less frequently, than we did when we lived in the city.

A newspaper interview with Sang Ye said he was struck by the 'eerie silence' of Canberra. He was mystified by the fact that people did not strip the edible berries from trees lining the avenues there, or shoot the wild duck he saw on the lake. It took him a few months before he realised Australians weren't necessarily so stupid after all: 'I began to understand how people treat each other here, and how they treat animals too – live and let live.' I like to think this is, by and large, true. In a world filled with fanaticism and suspicion, it means we do have something precious to offer, apart from the land we so unceremoniously appropriated. We have great need to hang on to this. To look no further than the situation of our children in school: it is no longer simply a question of Australians allowing migrants to fit into the community – in some city areas the situation has been reversed, with Vietnamese, Chinese, or Greek students forming an over-whelming majority. An important help with solving such conflicts is that the country does offer space, there is little of that terrible sense of having nowhere to go, no room to move.

We ourselves are very well off in this regard. Our house stands on seven acres along the side of a headland, backed by several hundred acres of wild bush. It is built of timber, with a stone wall at either end; quite a modern looking place, sitting low to the ground, unpretentious and very liveable. Part of it we built, including the lounge room with its stone fireplace and the terrace at the back where we have a barbecue for outdoor eating on summer evenings (there is nothing unusual in this, Australians very commonly build their houses and do their own renovations). Our Sydney friends were amazed when we moved here. 'Won't you feel out of touch?' they said. But that's what people in London say about going to live in Sydney. Of course we are not out of touch. All one needs to break is an attitude: the metropolitan attitude – which is a colonial attitude too – of thinking there is only one centre. We have wonderful neighbours living about a kilometre away. Life is pretty well as perfect as our failings allow it to be. The house faces slightly east of north (the sunniest of all aspects), looking across a vast expanse of ocean in the direction, roughly speaking, of Alaska.

It could scarcely be much further removed from the tunnel formed by a settee-back pushed against the piano keyboard in that flat above a garage in Russell Street, Stroud, with the occasional bomb going off and a sheet of flame rising in the night at the rear of the building where an old fuel storage shed was hit by incendiaries. Yet somehow it feels all of a piece with the exotic land of my grandparents' farm at Kangaroo Valley, the land I once glimpsed in old snapshots. The sheer size of the ocean on one hand and the forest on the other, the lack of any building to be seen, the prevalent concern with wildlife (though in our generation, we are more keen to preserve animals than hunt them), the outdoor lifestyle ... these things do add up, in a way, to a modern version of what I vaguely expected when setting sail from Tilbury almost forty years ago.

So Bet and I sat looking at the view north along the coastline, with Mount Dromedary rising on the horizon. Later in the afternoon, this wooded mountain top, which has probably never known a flake of snow, remained bathed in sunlight well after the beach lay in the shadow of evening. Dromedary was another of the mountains named by Captain

182

Cook in 1770. Characteristically, Cook's maps of the coast charted nothing but those fragments which he was able to record in some detail; he declined to indulge in guesswork. His maps were admirably accurate. But they were fragmentary also; and this was what made them so tantalising. They invited other explorers to seek further, to fill in the gaps and come to know more of what was, to the Europeans of the time, the last great unknown land.

I, too, in my own way, have presented an incomplete Australia. In my travels I have seen a lot, but I know it is only a fraction of the riches offered by this wonderful country. The fascination is inexhaustible. The journey has not finished. I look forward to much more to come.

SUGGESTED READING LIST

History and Social Commentary

Carter, Paul, *The Road to Botany Bay*, Faber & Faber, London, 1987.

Clark, C. M. H., *Sources of Australian History*, Oxford University Press, London, 1957.

Dallas, K. M., *Trading Posts or Penal Colonies*, Fullars Bookshop, Hobart, 1969.

Denholm, David, *The Colonial Australians*, Penguin, Melbourne, 1979.

Dunn, Michael, *Australia and the Empire*, Fontana, Sydney, 1984.

Gilbert, Kevin, *Because a White Man'll Never Do It*, Angus & Robertson, Sydney, 1973.

Hughes, Robert, *The Fatal Shore*, Collins, London, 1986.

McQueen, Humphrey, *A New Britannia*, Penguin, Melbourne, 1986.

—, *Gallipoli to Petrov*, Allen & Unwin, Sydney, 1984.

Reynolds, Henry, *The Other Side of the Frontier*, Penguin, Melbourne, 1982.

Symons, Michael, *One Continuous Picnic*, Penguin, Melbourne, 1984.

Wright, Judith, *The Cry for the Dead*, Oxford University Press, Melbourne, 1982.

Reference Books

Cameron, Angus. *The Second Australian Almanac*, Angus & Robertson, Sydney, 1986.

Wild, Hooton, and Andrews, *The Oxford Companion to Australian Literature,* Oxford University Press, Melbourne, 1985.

Wilkes, G. A., *A Dictionary of Australian Colloquialisms,* Fontana, Melbourne, 1980.

Photograph Books

Cox, Philip, and Stacey, Wesley, *Historic Towns of Australia,* Lansdowne, Melbourne, 1983.

—, *Rude Timber Buildings in Australia,* Thames & Hudson, London, 1969; Angus & Robertson, Sydney, 1980.

Isaacs, Jennifer (ed.), *Australian Dreaming: 40,000 Years of Aboriginal History,* Lansdowne, Sydney, 1980.

Moore, David, and Hall, Rodney. *Australia: Image of a Nation,* Collins, Sydney, 1983.

Tweedie, Penny, *This Is My Country,* Collins, Sydney, 1985.

Novels

Astley, Thea, *It's Raining in Mango,* Putnam, New York, 1988.

Barnard Eldershaw, M., *Tomorrow and Tomorrow and Tomorrow,* Virago, London, 1983.

Boyd, Martin, *When Blackbirds Sing,* Penguin, Melbourne, 1984.

Castro, Brian, *Birds of Passage,* Allen & Unwin, Sydney, 1983.

Foster, David, *The Pure Land,* Penguin, Melbourne, 1985.

Hall, Rodney, *Just Relations,* Penguin, London, 1984.

—, *Kisses of the Enemy,* Penguin, Melbourne, 1987.

Malouf, David, *12 Edmonstone Street,* Penguin, London, 1986.

Moorhouse, Frank, *The Everlasting Secret Family,* Angus & Robertson, Sydney, 1980.

Murnane, Gerald, *Landscape with Landscape*, Penguin, Melbourne, 1987.

Richardson, Henry Handel, *The Getting of Wisdom*, Virago, London, 1982.

White, Patrick, *The Tree of Man*, Penguin, London, 1956.

—, *Voss,* Penguin, London, 1963.

Winton, Tim, *That Eye the Sky*, Penguin, Melbourne, 1986.

Poetry

Adamson, Robert, *Where I Come From*, Big Smoke Books, Sydney, 1979.

Dransfield, Michael, *Collected Poems*, University of Queensland Press, Brisbane, 1987.

Hall, Rodney (ed.), *The Collins Book of Australian Poetry*, Collins, Sydney, 1984.

Harwood, Gwen, *Selected Poems*, Angus & Robertson, Sydney, 1975.

Murray, Les A., *Selected Poems*, Angus & Robertson, Sydney, 1976.

Shapcott, Thomas W., *Shabbytown Calendar*, University of Queensland Press, Brisbane, 1987.

Tranter, John, *Crying in Early Infancy*, Makar Press, Brisbane, 1977.

Tsaloumas, Dimitris, *Contemporary Australian Poetry*, University of Queensland Press, Brisbane, 1986.

Wright, Judith, *Alive,* Angus & Robertson, Sydney, 1973.

INDEX

Aborigines: arts, 40–1, 50, 74, 103, 130–1, 138, 142–4, *pl. 9, 22, 23*; attitude to, 140–1; corroborees, 50, 137; culture, 39–50, 142; dance, 74, 137; diet, 139–40; land rights, 4–6, 42–3, 44, 139–41; land use, 39; mythology, 48–50, 75, 103, 129–30; Northern Territory, 139–41; numbers, 40; oral history, 42–3; origins, 40; package holidays among, 148; prescribed territory, 37; as 'problem', 44–5; purchases, 146; religion, 37–9, 103; Tasmanian, 89; technology, 45; tribal councils, 43; tribal wars, 42
accent, Australian, 82
Adam, Robert, 82
Adelaide (SA), 94; art gallery, 103; Cooper's Brewery, 97; desert hinterland, 102; Festival, 94–5; weather, 55, 99; wines, 95–6
adventure, finding, 105
agriculture, difficult, 50–5
air travel, domestic, 51–5
Albany (WA), 113–15
Alice Springs (NT), 144–7
Alligator River, 139
All Saints vineyard, Rutherglen (Vic), 58, 59–60
American immigrants, 146–7
Americas Cup yacht race, 120
Anglesea (Vic), 75
animals *see* wildlife
Ansell, Rod, 135

Anzac Day, 111–14
Armidale (NSW), Saumarez residence, 28–9
Arnhem Land (NT), 139, 141–2, *pl. 2*
ashrams, 166–7
'Ash Wednesday' (1983), 68
Australia Day, 111
Australian Ballet, 74
Australian Capital Territory (ACT), 173
Australian Rules Football, 71, *pl. 25*
autumn: colour, 62–3; weather, 36, 176
Ayer's Rock/Uluru (NT), 3–6, 49–50, 145

Balfour Report (1926), 171–2
Ballarat (Vic), 63–6, 70; Sovereign Hill, 63–5
ballet, 74
bark paintings, 50, 103, 131, 142–3, *pl. 9*
Barragga Bay (NSW), 178, 180, 181–2
Bass Strait, 84
beach life, 16, 18, 19–21
Beechworth (Vic), 58, 60–1, 63, *pl. 16*
beer, Australian, 97
Beerwah, Mount (Qld), 166
Bega Valley (NSW), 179
Bendigo (Vic), 61–2, 63, 70, *pl. 6*
Binna Burra (Qld), 165
Bishop, John, 95
bites, poisoned, 132–3, 134

187

Index

Index

190

Index

Murray River, 56–8
Murrumbidgee Irrigation Scheme, 58
myrtle forest, 90–1

Namatjira, Albert, 41, 143–4
Nash, John, 82
national identity, 17, 22; *see also* personality
nature, observing, 57–8
New South Wales (NSW): floods, 160; forests, 23; railway gauge, 69; skiing, 174; surfing, 19; trees, 62
Normanton (Qld), 154
Northern Territory (NT), 136; climate, 36; powers, 140
Nowra, Louis, 74
Nullarbor Plain (SA/WA), 115–18

Obiri Rock (NT), 138–9
ocker, definition of, 12
octopus, blue-ringed, 134
Olga, Mount, group (NT), 145, *pl. 31*
opal mines, 104, 105
Oscar Ranges (WA), 122
Otway Ranges (Vic), bushfires, 68
Ovens River Valley (Vic), 62
Overland Track (Tas), 90–1

paddle-steamer trips, 57–8
paper industries, 119
Papunya (NT), paintings, 143
peppermint gum forests, 119
Perisher Valley ski resort (NSW), 174, 175
Perroux, Narelle, 177
personality, Australian, 23, 55, 69, 126–9, 135–6, 141, 167–8, 181
Perth (WA), 119–20; sunshine, 35
Petrie, Andrew, 42
Petrie, Tom, 42
Phillip, Arthur, Governor, 6
pilliga scrub, 29
Pinnacles Desert (WA), 122, 123–4
place names, 75–6

platypuses, 77–8
Pope, Alexander, 82
Port Arthur (Tas), 83, 84; *pl. 13*
Port Augusta (SA), 103
Port Campbell National Park (Vic), 76
Port Fairy (Vic), 76
Pottinger, Sir Frederick, 31
Princetown (Vic), 76
prisons, early, 83–4, 91, *pl. 13*
property and power, 81
Public Services, 101–2

Queensland (Qld): agriculture, 152, 166; climate, 35–6; domestic architecture, 155–8; immigrants, 167; motels, 152–4; railway gauge, 69; roads, 156; surfing beaches, 19; tropical rainforests, 67
Queenstown (Tas), 91

rabbits, problems of, 116
race relations, 167; *see also* immigrants
railway gauge, differences in, 69
rain, 36
rainforest, 154
Rams Head Range, Snowy Mountains, *pl. 30*
Ravenshoe (Qld), 153–4
Ravenswood (Qld), 150–2, *pl. 15*
Rayleigh Scattering, 22
Recruiting Officer, The (Farquhar) 82
red-back spider, 132
religious tolerance, 167
Reynolds, Henry, 48
Reynolds, Sir Joshua, 82
Richmond (Tas), 84–7, *pl. 14*; bridge, 86–7; Prospect House, 87; St Luke's Church, 86
rivalry, inter-state, 69–70
rivers, 36; flooding, 66–7, 160
river travel, 57–8
rural life, 180–2
Rutherglen (Vic), vineyard, 58, 59–60, *pl. 17*

191

Index

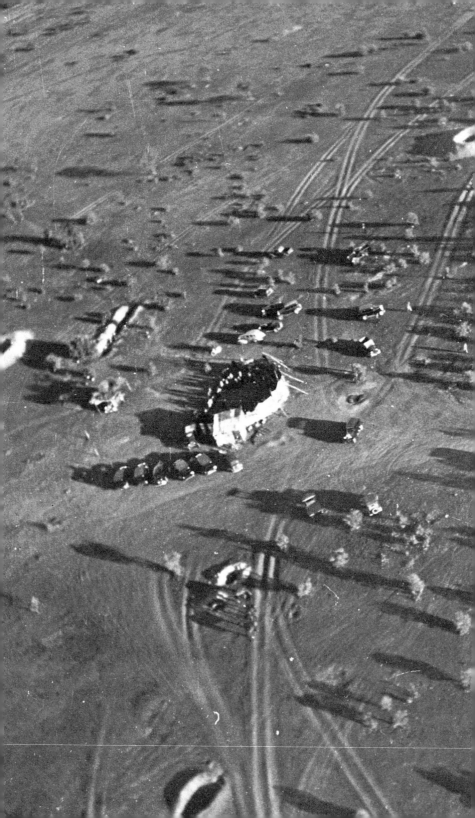